T0359571

Printed on Stone
The Lithographs of Charles Troedel

Includes *The Melbourne Album*

Printed on Stone
The Lithographs of Charles Troedel

Includes *The Melbourne Album*

Amanda Scardamaglia

M

MELBOURNE BOOKS

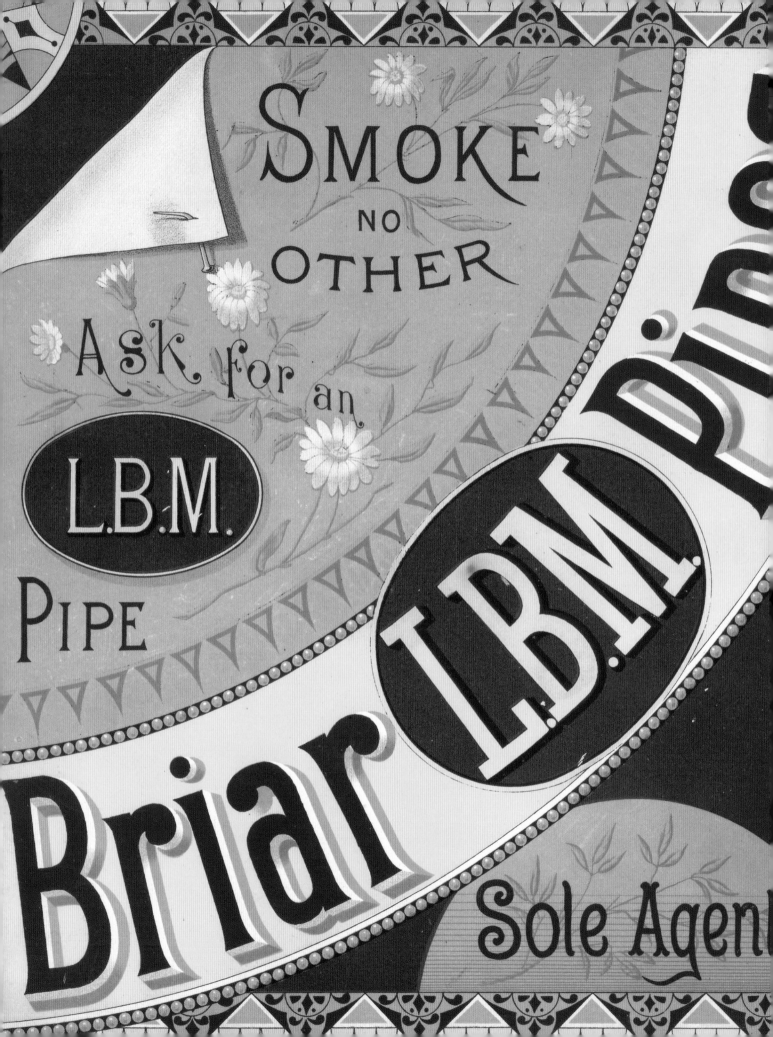

LEVY BROS & Cᵒ MELBOURNE.

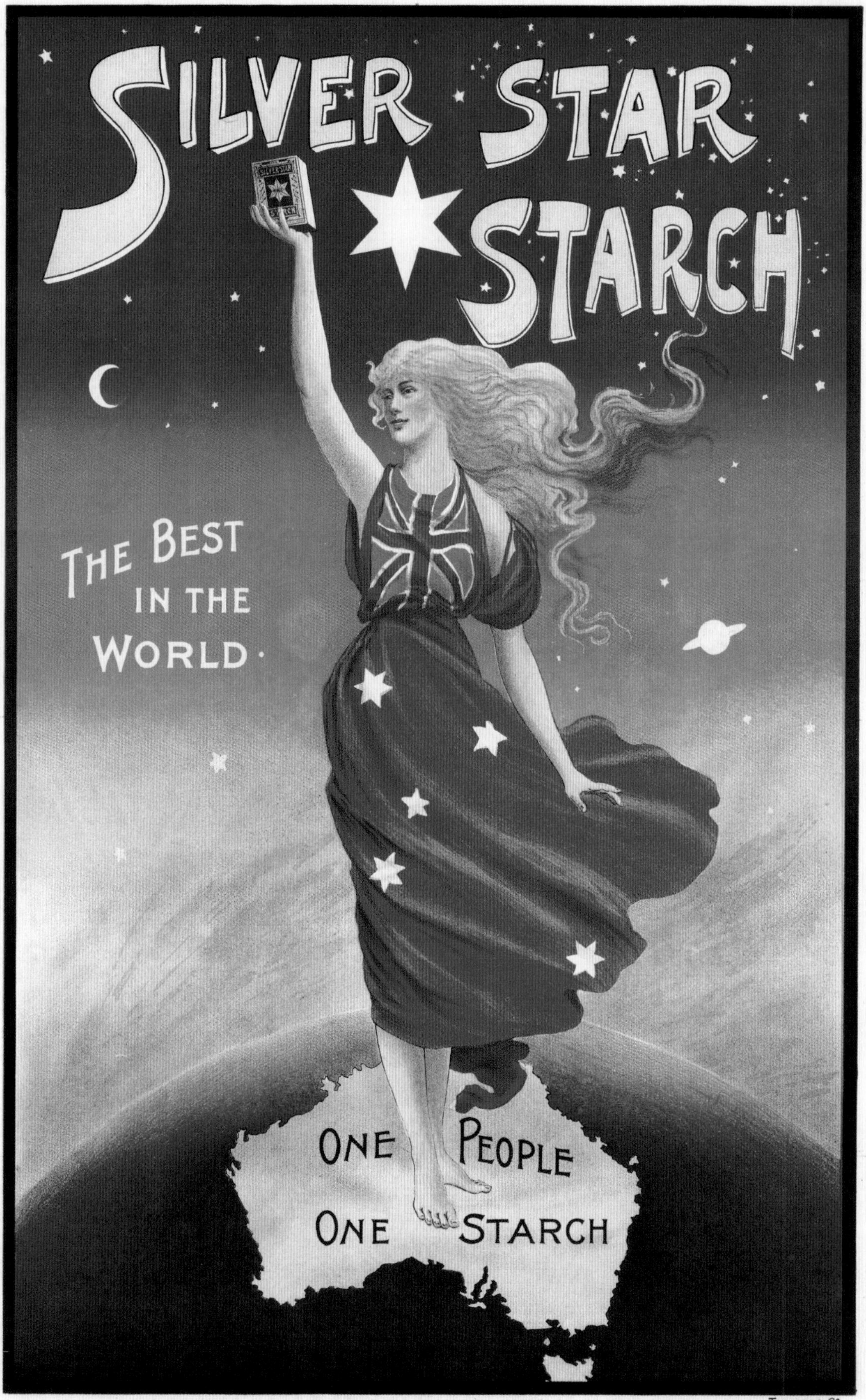

Acknowledgements

Charles Troedel featured as little more than a footnote in my PhD thesis. More than a decade later, his life and his work is documented in full, in this book, thanks to a long list of people.

From Stone to Print would not have been possible without the support of a State Library Victoria Creative Fellowship (2015-2016). I am immensely grateful to the SLV team, who assisted me during the Fellowship and thereafter. Thanks to Gail Schmidt, Margot Jones, Olga Tsara, Lucas Manuell. A very special thanks to Gerard Hayes from the Picture Collection, who provided me access to the Troedel Archive, and assisted me while rummaging through the nearly 10,000 items in the SLV collection.

Thanks to my colleagues in Australia and around the world for their generous feedback on this project in its various stages. Thanks to my wonderful Swinburne Law School colleagues. Thanks also to those who commented on my work at the Faculty of Law at Uppsala University, Sweden (2016), at La Trobe Law School at La Trobe University (2016), at CIPPM at Bournemouth University, England (2017), at the Art in Law in Art Conference at University of Western Australia (2017), at the Australasian Intellectual Property Academics Conference at the University of Sydney (2017), and at ISHTIP in Rome, Italy (2018). Thanks also to Claudy Op den Kamp, whose aesthetic vision elevated this idea into something tangible.

Thanks to Uppsala University, Sweden and especially Marianna Dahlén for supporting me as a visiting scholar in 2016 and giving me the gift of time to work on this project. Thanks also to CIPPM at Bournemouth University and especially Maurizio Borghi and Dinusha Mendis who supported my Short-Term Residential Fellowship in 2017, which allowed me to focus on writing my manuscript.

Thanks to Melbourne Books, and my publisher David Tenenbaum, for believing in this project and bringing this remarkable story to life. Thanks to Marianna Berek-Lewis for her design work, and for showcasing this spectacular collection of images in all of their glory. Thanks also to my trusted research assistant, Cheng Voung. And to those who lived through this book and experienced the highs and lows with me – Julie Scardamaglia, Mitchell Adams, Catherine Bond, Vicki Huang, Jason Bosland – thank you, thank you, thank you.

A final word of thanks must go to the Troedel family, especially Bill Troedel and Alastair Troedel. Your enthusiasm and support has been all encompassing, and I am especially grateful for that. It has been a pleasure and a privilege to write this book, and share your family history.

This book is dedicated to my parents, thank you, for everything.

Amanda Scardamaglia

> *Victory Bitters*
> (c 1872)
> State Library Victoria,
> H96.160/2131

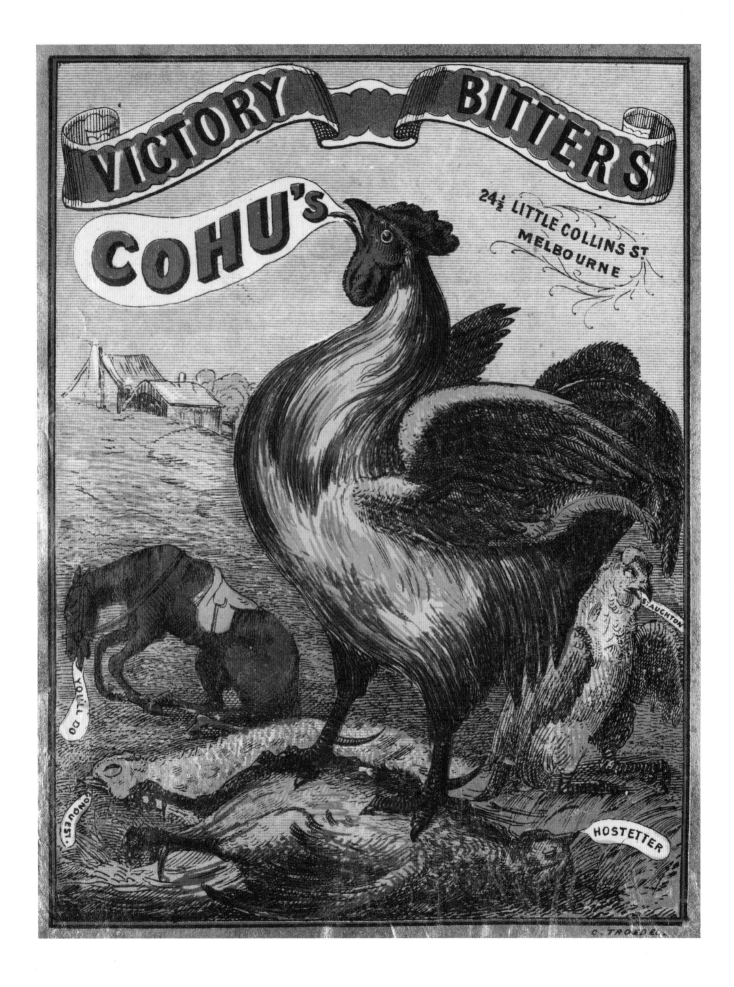

9

'Standard' Cushion Head Lining
(c 1880–1890)
State Library Victoria,
H2000.180/223

Foreword

What led to the success of Charles Troedel and the business he founded?

The political upheavals occurring in Europe at the time, in particular, the unification of Prussia and surrounding states into the nation we now know of as Germany, let the young Charles to look elsewhere.

Alternatively, was it the development of the Industrial Revolution in Europe and the Americas, and the development of railways. It is stated that the most successful business people of all time, for example Andrew Carnegie and John D Rockerfeller, built their businesses in different ways during the second half of the nineteenth century, but used the development of the railways in the 1860s as their foundation. Certainly, the early development of Charles Troedel's business was in the production of posters for the railway stations and carriages around Melbourne. This is the time when colourful display advertising had its genesis.

The discovery of gold and the development of mining in Australia, and particularly in Victoria, during the mid 19th century, added rapid development and opportunity to the fledgling colony, making Melbourne reputedly the richest, and one of the fastest growing cities in the world.

The building of the city of Melbourne provided opportunities for general printing for fledgling businesses and the developing bureaucracy, which Charles Troedel was well placed to service.

Charles was regarded as a first class tradesman and surrounded himself with the very best artists and lithographers, many of whom are revered today in the art world. The firm's work is regarded now as being of the highest artistic quality.

The boom fuelled by gold, and supported by wool exports 'home' to England, lasted through to the 1890s when depression hit. By this time Charles had expanded his business to Sydney with the help of his new business partner, Edward Cooper. They survived the economic hardships partly by divesting themselves of the Sydney business.

Into the twentieth century, we find similar opportunities being recognised and utilised.

For instance, Charles' grandson, Theo, developed label printing expertise based on the need for canned food for the armed forces, and subsequently for exports of canned food to the United Kingdom. By the mid 1950s Troedel and Cooper Pty Ltd were printing 80% of the can labels produced in Australia, using techniques which were subsequently copied around the world.

So was it recognising the economic and political uncertainties and opportunities, being in the right place at the right time, attracting the most skilled with whom to work, producing the highest quality, or just plain good luck? Maybe it was all of these factors.

Amanda, on behalf of the Troedel Family we congratulate you on your years of research on this project. Your work, which was centred on the State Library of Victoria Troedel Collection highlights how the printing industry in Melbourne became a leader on the world stage.

Alastair Troedel

Introduction

∧
*Mr Frank Thornton's
5th Australasian Tour.
On a Wave of Laughter*
(c 1890-1895)
State Library Victoria,
H2000.180/45

Charles Troedel was a master printer and lithographer. He was also the face behind the production of much of Australia's earliest surviving printed material including advertising posters, product labels, and other ephemera.

These works provide a graphic history of nineteenth century Australia, speaking to the prevailing state of commerce, culture, social trends and colonial norms. Inexplicably, Troedel's role in the production of this capsule history has been overlooked by art, design and social historians. Also overlooked is the legal dimension to this history, and the fact that his work, and lithography more generally, was responsible for transforming advertising in nineteenth century Australia – having a profound impact on the way these commercial works were protected and regulated. Until now.

This book provides a history of advertising in Australia. It uses Troedel's catalogue of lithographs to trace the production and evolution of nineteenth century Australian advertising – in the home, at the bar, in health, hygiene and housework, with style and fashion and in leisurely pursuits. The book starts from the proposition that technological arrangements heavily mediate the social relations in all societies. Technology, therefore, as a form of social organisation, is a key player in society and culture.[1]

Lithography was the key technological arrangement mediating nineteenth century colonial Australian society, with stone press printing transforming the production of graphical and visual arts in Australia in the same way that the printing press transformed the written word centuries earlier. These graphical prints and advertisements were carriers of meaning and ideology, leaving a profound, and yet unexplored, cultural legacy. This book uncovers the legacy of the lithograph and examines how lithography, as embodied in the Troedel archive, both mirrored early colonial Australian culture and society but also created it. The book also pays homage to Troedel's significant contribution to this process, and his contribution to nineteenth century Australian art more generally.

It borrows from the traditions of legal history and cultural history. The book is primarily concerned with signs, symbols and semiotics – inspired by the works of Swiss linguist Ferdinand de Saussure and the long list of modern semiotic scholars who followed.[2] With a focus on the objects in the Troedel archive,[3] this book uses content analysis, which is typically used to analyse art, illustrations, advertising material and its meaning.[4] It also uses synchronic analysis, as a method to examine the messages contained within these objects. These tools are used to uncover differences in communication content across the colonies and the British Empire, identify propaganda and government rhetoric in advertising and unmask the attitudinal and behavioural responses to advertising during the nineteenth century in Australia.[5] The legal response to these narratives are also examined.

A history such as this is only possible because of the thorough and well-preserved archive documenting the life and legacy of Charles Troedel and his firm Troedel & Co. At the heart of this archive are the corporate records of the Troedel printing business, which was founded in 1863. The records span over a century and were donated to the State Library of Victoria in 1968. Together with the prior holdings of material produced by Troedel and held in the Picture Collection of the State Library of Victoria,[6] the Troedel archive is the most comprehensive print archive to survive in a public collection in Australia.[7]

The records contained in the archive are the product of the meticulous record-keeping of Arthur Hewett. Hewett spent his entire career and more than 65 years with Troedel & Co. His time at the firm started in December 1887, when he abandoned a scholarship to take up the job of office boy. Hewett had been involved in all of the administrative aspects of the printing business, holding the role of secretary and director. On his retirement at age 79 in 1963, Hewett remarked upon how of all the things that had changed in his years, they also remained the same: '[w]hen I started work in the offices in Flinders Lane, the firm employed about the same number of men as now – 150 to 160 – but production today is infinitely greater.'[8]

The Troedel archive contains more than 9,000 copies of printed works produced by the company. The printed works are collated in 22 albums and displayed thematically, and as such, the date of production and details of authorship is not always obvious. The albums were originally collated as scrap books and include fold-outs of larger printed items. The categories of works include postage stamps, invitations, letterheads and corporate and personalised stationery, event and theatre programmes, promotional pamphlets and brochures, as well as company share certificates. The collection also includes an eclectic selection of newspaper clippings and election cards.

It further includes some of Troedel & Co's own stationary, including promotional posters, trade cards, business cards, letterheads, calendars, invoice books and order books used to complete order requests and track printing jobs. A major part of the collection includes labels, trade marks and advertising posters which were themselves thematically organised including collections for jams, preserved fruits, alcohol, soaps and candles, tea and coffee, tobacco, sauces and condiments. A series of more than 400 advertising posters was also preserved. The State Library of Victoria also holds several additional boxes of miscellaneous items.

This book brings these print specimens and the Troedel archive into the public gaze for the first time. It presents these works across a number of themes representing the different aspects of nineteenth century culture and colonial Australian society. These themes cut across private and public life, the individual and the State and are collated here with one simple objective – to provide a history of Australian advertising in the nineteenth century through the lens of the lithograph – a history *printed on stone*.

Illustration of Charles Troedel's
Occupation and Address (1870)
State Library Victoria,
H96.160/1387

Awarded First Prize, Melbourne
International Exhibition (1881)
State Library Victoria,
H96.160/2078

I
The Visual Century

∧

The Australasian Illustrated Weekly (c 1881-1890)
State Library Victoria,
H2000.212/11

Charles Troedel was remembered as one of '... Melbourne's pioneer printers ...' and '... the leading exponent of the lithography branch of the trade.'[1] He was generous in his craft, sharing his knowledge at the service of his friends.[2] Above all, Troedel was a '... genial and courteous gentleman ...' who was dedicated to his family and popular among his friends.[3]

Troedel's brilliant career as printmaker, craftsman, and publisher began as a child when he was an apprentice lithographer to his father Carl Auguste Troedel at age 13. Some years later in 1859, after working in Norway and London, Troedel caught the attention of Norwegian printer Augustus William Schuhkrafft who was visiting Europe with a brief to recruit staff for his Melbourne printing business. Schuhkrafft engaged Troedel and Richard Wendel, a gifted lithographic artist and draftsman. It was a decision that would set Troedel upon the path of a long and prosperous career in printing.

Born Johannes Theodor Carl Troedel (26 June 1835-31 October 1906) in Hamburg, Germany, Charles Troedel as he was known, was the son of Carl Auguste Troedel (Trödel) and Maria Troedel (née Buck). Troedel travelled to Australia on a Danish passport and arrived in Melbourne on the *Great Britain* on 5 February 1860 at Hobson's Bay in Williamstown.[4] He then took up a position at Schuhkrafft's Wholesale Paper Bag Manufacturing and Printing Establishment, a firm best known for printing many of the flyers for the early subdivisions of land in Melbourne. His experience at Schuhkrafft's proved invaluable, and upon finishing his apprenticeship, Troedel set up a small workshop on Collins Street in Melbourne in June 1863. It was here that Troedel & Co, master printers and lithographers was born.

The workshop was opposite *The Argus* office in an area that was then considered the Golden Mile of the city and is now the site of the Melbourne Town Hall.[5] The business moved location several times. In one instance, the move was necessitated by fire, which had gutted Troedel's printing facilities on Flinders Lane.[6] Throughout all of this, the operation remained in the family. After Troedel's death in 1906, his son Walter took over the business, who went into partnership with Edward Cooper, and the firm was renamed Troedel & Copper. The business was sold and taken over several times thereafter. Even so, Walter's son Theodore, his son William (Bill), and later Bill together with his son Alastair were all involved at various stages, in some capacity. It was not until 2013 that the firm went into liquidation, bringing to a close a monumental 150 year run of the printing business bearing the Troedel name.

It is remarkable that Troedel was able to build such a successful enterprise in Australia, using a printing method that was uniquely European, with German roots. Troedel migrated to Australia at a time when a large number of immigrants, including many German Lutherans, were arriving in Australia from Prussia. Most of these migrants settled in South Australia and Queensland, where their work ethic was applauded.[7]

In Victoria, the first German immigrants arrived under a British bounty to attract vineyard workers.[8] Others moved to Victoria to set up missions to serve the local indigenous inhabits.[9] Hundreds more rushed to Victoria hoping to strike gold and by 1861, the Germans had become the largest non-British population in Victoria, numbering 10,000.[10]

The wave of German immigration to the Australian colonies also included young students and members of the liberal middle class who were looking to leave Germany following the failed 1848 uprisings, which had resulted in political upheaval and the suppression of dissent. Many of them went to the United States, while others made the long journey to Australia. In Victoria, this included educated artists and scientists such as Ferdinand von Mueller, who became the highly influential director of Melbourne's Botanic Gardens and a close companion of Troedel.

The fact that Troedel and others like him moved from Germany to work abroad attests to the favourable conditions awaiting free settlers in Australia. Here, Troedel was able to pursue his interest in lithography, free from the patent limitations his European counterparts were constrained by.[11] He was also able to take advantage of the technical expertise and know-how he had acquired in Europe, which was in short supply and high demand in the growing colonies. When you add Troedel's work ethic and passion for printing to the mix, it was clear that Troedel was destined to achieve great things in Australia.

Photographer unknown, *Johannes Theodore Carl (Charles) Troedel and Julia Sarah Troedel (nee Glover and their family)* (c 1895)
Troedel Family Archive

Photographer unknown, *Employees of Charles Troedel & Co. March 1899* (1889)
State Library Victoria,
H2011.190a

Photographer unknown, *Employees
of Charles Troedel & Co. March 1899*
(1889)
State Library Victoria,
H2011.190b

∨
Photographer unknown, *Employees
of Charles Troedel & Co March 1899*
(1889)
State Library Victoria,
H2011.190c

Early Life and Work

Troedel was a good-natured man who was admired by those who knew and worked with him, as evident in the recollections of his contemporaries. He was also fiercely devoted to his family. On 29 June 1869 at age 33, Troedel married Julia Sarah Glover at St Paul's Church of England in Melbourne. The wedding celebrations were attended by family, friends and colleagues, and the event was even reported in the newspaper.[12] Together, Charles and Julia had four sons – Walter Albert, Rudolph August, Ferdinand George, Charles Arthur Robert – and two daughters Julie Alice (Dolly) and Elsa Sylvia. Troedel's wife and children were all involved in the business during his life and after his death.

Troedel also treated those who were a part of the business like they were family. This reciprocity was clearly demonstrated at the company's annual social party, where Troedel's family and colleagues celebrated their successes and friendship together. Here, Troedel (who had just returned from Europe) was presented '... with a handsomely illuminated address, containing portraits of all the employees in the establishment, and also a diamond bracelet to Mrs. Troedel.[13] Following a toast by the firm's manager, William Colley and [a]fter drinking the health of Mr. and Mrs. Troedel, dancing was kept up for the remainder of the evening.'[14]

Troedel's first and most notable work, which set him up for later success, was 'The Melbourne Album', a compilation of prints depicting views of Melbourne' and its surrounding districts.[15] Save for two prints, the album was produced and printed by Troedel at his Collins Street workshop between 1863 and 1864, which in time became known as the Melbourne Album Office. Troedel used sedimentary limestone imported from Bavaria to print the album, which despite its cost, was selected because of its high quality.[16] This preference set Troedel apart from other printers, as many of his competitors used cheaper, inferior product.

The popularity of 'The Melbourne Album' was such that in 1878, Troedel & Co produced the 'New South Wales Album' out of the newly established Sydney office.[17] For this album, Troedel collaborated with Richard Wendel (sometimes attributed to Robert Wendel), who drew all of the lithographs in the collection. This album comprised 24 coloured chromolithographic plates, each with a printed caption. Troedel and Wendel went on to have a long and rich professional relationship, with Wendel producing the artwork for many of the theatre posters manufactured by the firm.

Troedel's chief collaborator on 'The Melbourne Album' was François Cogné, who produced 12 of the drawings in the 24 plate collection, and possibly another four which were marked anonymous. Cogné was an artist and French teacher who in 1859 produced the 'Ballarat Album', a collection of 16 lithographic views of Ballarat, all based on photographs taken by William Bardwell. He proposed the idea of a Melbourne themed album to Troedel based on his earlier work, having first met Troedel during his time with Schuhkrafft. Troedel agreed to take part in the project after Cogné promised it would be a financial success. The series was foreshadowed in *The Argus* in 1863, and shortly thereafter, it became a reality.[18]

Nicholas Chevalier was another contributor to 'The Melbourne Album', with two prints derived from his paintings *Wentworth River Diggins* (1863) and *Mount Abrupt and the Grampians* (1864) included in the compilation. He paired with Troedel again in 1865, producing 'N Chevalier's Album of Chromolithographs'. Chevalier (1828-1902) was born in Saint Petersburg and studied painting in Lausanne and architecture in Munich before moving to London where he experienced some success in lithography and watercolour. He moved to Melbourne in 1855, and after visiting the gold mines, he began working for the newly established *Melbourne Punch* and *Illustrated Australian News*.

Some of the first lithographs produced for sale as part of 'The Melbourne Album' were *Collins Street* (1863) and *Dight's Mill* (1863), both drawn by Cogné. These were published at Schuhkrafft's and were advertised in *The Argus* with a monthly subscription (for two views), to be completed in 12 monthly parts for the price of 7s 6d.[19] *Collins*

Street (1863) shows a '... sedate and dignified thoroughfare with much of the character that it has now.'[20] At the forefront of the picture, to the right is the Union Bank of Australia, which went on to amalgamate with the Bank of Australasia and become the Australia and New Zealand Bank in 1950. The Criterion Hotel is also shown on the same side, being the south side of the street. On the left of the frame, on the north side of the street, is the then newly built Bank of New South Wales. Into the distance are Scot's tower and the Old Treasury Building, which was built from 1859 to 1862 and designed by architect J J Clark.

Dight's Mill (1863) shows the property of Dight's Mill, which was located on the banks of the Yarra River and served as a source of power for Dight brothers John and Charles who operated the business.[21] The mill was built at Yarra Falls, in Yarra Bend Park (near Studley Park) after John Dight purchased the block of land in 1839. Dight had already established a flour milling business near Campbell Town in New South Wales but left for Victoria where he constructed the mill in 1841 using bricks from Tasmania. The Dight family sold the mill to Edwin Trennery in 1878 and the land was later subdivided.[22]

The remaining 22 prints in the series were developed and printed at Troedel's Melbourne Album Office. The significance of 'The Melbourne Album' is still recognised to this day. A new limited edition with textual matter was published in 1961, to mark the century since Troedel first arrived in Australia. It was commissioned by the Troedel family and edited by Clive Turnbull who included a preface about the collection.[23] In 1962, the National Gallery of Victoria exhibited 'The Melbourne Album' to celebrate the 100 year anniversary of the arrival of Troedel to Australia. This was cause for inspiration for artist Harold Freedman, who embarked upon drawing Melbourne from the same vantage points as depicted in 'The Melbourne Album' 100 years earlier. Six of these lithographs were published by Griffin Press. Others are held in the Picture Collection of the State Library of Victoria.[24]

Thanks to the success of 'The Melbourne Album', Troedel's trade proliferated, and he commenced operations in Sydney trading as C Troedel & Co in 1887. It was here that he produced the 'New South Wales Album'. It was also at this time that Troedel's long-time friend and business associate Edward Cooper became more involved in the business. Cooper started at the firm in 1872 at age 13 to assist with the accounts. By the time

Cooper was 21, he was left to manage the business on his own while Troedel went overseas on business.[25]

Cooper officially joined the business in 1887 and in 1890, he and Troedel formed a partnership. During this period, Cooper moved to Sydney to run their subsidiary operation, but the move was short-lived. After five years and following the depression and great crash of the 1890s, the firm closed and Cooper returned to Melbourne. Cooper nevertheless continued to play an integral role in the venture and following Troedel's death, he carried on the business with Troedel's sons.[26]

While 'The Melbourne Album' and its companion, the 'New South Wales Album', were marque publications of their time, they were among many lithographic prints produced in Australia during that period. Over the next half-century, lithography became the premier means of print production in Australia for both artistic and commercial printing, a century after the printing method had established itself in Europe. And while lithography only had a limited effect on printmaking early on in Europe, by the time lithographic presses reached Australian shores, the technology had matured to such an extent that its impact in Australia was immediate.

Richard Wendel (1851-1926),
Middle Harbour, Sydney, New South Wales (1878)
Published by Troedel & Co, Lithographers, Sydney
State Library Victoria, 30328102131777/7

MIDDLE HARBOUR,
SYDNEY, NEW SOUTH WALES

Richard Wendel (1851-1926),
Botanical Gardens (Farm Cove), Government House in Distance (1878)
Published by Troedel & Co, Lithographers, Sydney
State Library Victoria, 30328102131777/3

BOTANICAL GARDENS (FARM COVE)
GOVERNMENT HOUSE IN DISTANCE.

Connecting the Mechanical and the Modern

Lithography (from Ancient Greek λίθος, lithos, meaning 'stone', and γράφειν, graphein, meaning 'to write') is a method of printing, typically using finely polished limestones, zinc or aluminium plates. To produce a lithograph, an artist draws on the surface of a limestone or other plate with greasy crayons, or a grease-like liquid ink such as touche. When the drawing is complete, a solution of gum arabic and nitric acid is washed across the stone. This fixes the grease to the stone and prevents it from further spreading or bleeding. The entire surface of the limestone is then washed with water, and the stone is rolled with the printing ink. Since grease and water repel each other, the ink adheres only to the greasy drawing and does not stick to the clean portions of the stone. Paper is then laid across the stone, and together they are pulled through a press. This transfers the image from the stone to the paper, producing a mirror image of the original image, completing the printing process.

Lithography has been described as having '... an intrinsic flexibility greater than any other medium employed by artists to make prints, responding with astonishing ease to the varying technical and stylistic demands made upon it.'[27] At the beginning of the nineteenth century '... chemical lithography challenged, and to some extent fractured, what are widely considered to be the salutary influences of typographic taste and convention.'[28] In short, lithography was a disruptive technology, and its impact was profound. Even so, its significance has been downplayed, crowded out by histories of Johannes Gutenberg's printing press and mechanical printing.

The nineteenth century was a period of drastic technological development in the visual world. Lithography was but one of several disruptive technologies to emerge during the visual century. Indeed, several image-making technologies were invented, including the panopticon, the panorama, the x-ray, cinema and photography.[29] These technologies brought with them significant social and legal consequences, which transformed the essential means in which we encounter the world, distorting perception and reality.[30] It was against this backdrop therefore, and in the midst of modernity, that the lithograph came to be.

Lithography was first discovered by Alois Senefelder (1771-1834) sometime around 1796 in Bavaria as an alternative to the existing printing processes using metal and wood engraving, which were both laborious and costly. It is a popular myth that Senefelder invented lithography by chance, based on a story about penning a list for his mother on a flat stone with a grease pencil, and on a hunch covered the surface with acid to discover that the greasy pencil protected the stone, revealing the list.[31] In reality, he was motivated to develop a cheap way to print his theatrical works, having become an accomplished playwright who struggled to pay the printing fees to reproduce his works.

The invention of lithography was prompted by the death of Senefelder's father. Some years earlier, Senefelder won a scholarship to study law at Ingolstadt in Bavaria, but when his father died when Senefelder was 20 years old, he left law school in order to support his mother and eight siblings writing plays. Senefelder's true passion was always the arts and he was never interested in studying law, having apparently only gone to law school at the behest of his father.

Whatever the circumstances of its invention, Senefelder was ultimately conferred exclusive printing rights for 15 years from the Prince of Bavaria on 3 September 1799 for 'Chemical Printing for Bavaria and the Electorate'.[32] Senefelder later worked with a well-known music publisher Johann Anton André from Offenbach in Germany where he set up a number of presses. In 1800, Senefelder followed Johann Anton André's brother Philipp to London to establish presses there too. In expanding his press empire, Senefelder was able to secure patent rights across Europe including in England, where he obtained a patent in 1801 for 'A New Method and Process of performing the Various Branches of the Art of Printing on Paper, Linen, Cotton, Woollen and other Articles'.[33]

Senefelder wrote about his patented process in 1818 in a handbook entitled *Vollstandiges Lehrbuch der Steindruckerei*. The text was translated and later published in English as *A Complete Course of Lithography and The Invention of Lithography*.[34] Here, Senefelder described the basic principles of lithography: '... it does not matter whether the lines be engraved or elevated, but the lines and points to be printed ought to be covered with a liquid [or chalk], to which the ink [for printing], consisting of a homogenous substance, must adhere according to its chemical affinity and the laws of attraction, while at the same time, all those places which are to remain blank, must possess the quality of repelling the colour ... All greasy substances ... do not unite with any watery liquid. On the contrary, they are inimical to water, and seem to repel it ... Upon this experience rests the whole foundation of this new method of printing ...'[35]

Senefelder's printing process quickly received attention from those interested in its commercial possibilities but also those attracted to its artistic potential. As such, lithography has a long and rich history in both commercial and artistic pursuits. Nevertheless, the place of lithography in history is understated. This is especially true in terms of the impact of lithography on advertising and branding practices. So, while lithography shares many similarities with the printing press in the way that it transformed society and evoked regulatory responses from government, it has not always been recognised as such, perhaps because '... in some ways the new process obeyed too well the rule that printing should be the unobtrusive servant of ideas...'[36]

While the technology of lithography has developed such that today, there are several types of lithographs, most of these methods still rely on the basic principles of Senefelder's process. The original lithographs, including those produced by Senefelder, were produced using black, greasy crayons but lithographic techniques evolved quickly to use more advanced methods and incorporate colour. One of the first advances was the tinted lithograph, which involved using one stone to print the original image, and subsequent stones to add colour to create atmospheric effects on the final print.

Another advance was photolithography, which allowed for the application of colour to photographs. Photolithography was purportedly developed by John Walter Osborne in Victoria, Australia. It allowed for the transfer of an image by a chemically-prepared negative imprinted by steam pressure directly on the lithographic stone. Osborne patented the process in Victoria in 1859, although his discovery was opposed by local lithographic draftsmen, engravers, and even photographers, who were fearful that his patent would ruin their callings.

An independent board appointed by the government to determine the originality and merits of the invention, recommended an immediate increase in Osborne's salary and contingent upon the free use of the process being ceded in perpetuity to the Victorian Government, he was granted £1000 in compensation.[37] There was still local resistance to the patent, which was thought to have been anticipated in Europe, even though it was accepted as an advance by some circles internationally. Osborne eventually found out that his process had in fact been previously patented, and was in use overseas.

The most notable and significant advance in lithography was chromolithography, which allowed for multi-coloured printing. While Senefelder presented the idea of coloured lithography and layering colour in *A Complete Course of Lithography* in 1818,[38] Franco-German Godefroy Engelmann is popularly credited with inventing it in around 1837.[39] Chromolithography was one of the first processes used for colour printing, where a separate stone was used for each colour, each having to pass through the press separately to produce the complete picture. The process initially involved three colour printing, but in principle, the number of colours that could be applied was infinite.

Lithography also played a role in the development of half-tone photographic reproduction. The layout of the lithographic book was also the precursor to modern book design. These developments meant that lithography attained the first stage of its maturation in just over a century between the years 1796 and 1905. Although its popularity was assisted by other improvements in production techniques including larger type sizes and new fonts, by the turn of the twentieth century, there was no doubt that lithography was an accepted part of printmaking.[40]

As a result, lithography was warmly embraced by artists, particularly in Europe and the United States. By the middle of the nineteenth century, lithography had become increasingly favoured for commercial use. In the 1890s, colour lithography became the predominate print form, assisted by the emergence of Jules Chéret, who is famed for his use of lithography and became a leading figure of the Belle Époque and the French poster art movement. Lithography's popularity was officially cemented when notable names including Pablo Picasso, Henri de Toulouse-Lautrec, Eugène Delacroix, Edgar Degas and Édouard Manet chose to work with lithographs at various times during their careers.

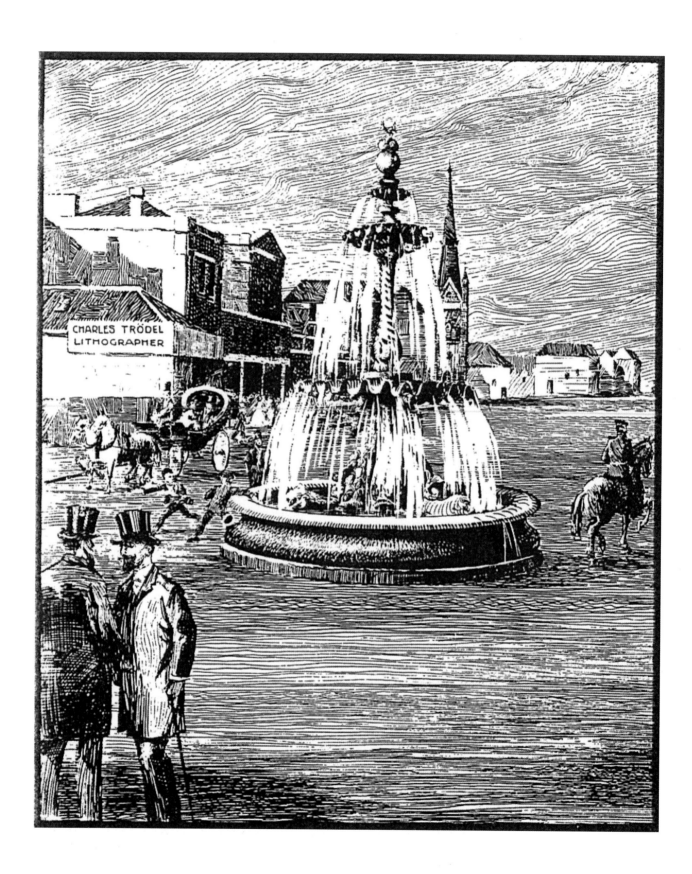

Lithography in Australia

There is no doubt that lithography was a uniquely European invention, with its early practice firmly rooted in Europe especially Germany and France. It was also popularly used in the United States to produce early advertising materials, and after the Civil War, colour lithography and chromolithography quickly became the printing medium of choice to reproduce convincingly real images.[41] In fact, the international copyright registers in the United States and the Stationers' Company records were littered with lithographs.[42] Somewhere in between is Australia.

The lithograph holds a special place in Australia. There are various reasons for this. One reason is connected to the idea that colonial territories were often treated as free zones where new techniques, processes, and instruments could be tried and tested by firms and bureaucracies, away from the limiting constraints of national populations, which were usually conservative and tied to old traditions and ideas. Where successful, these innovations could be sold back to the powers that be, inviting more investment and the possibility for the application of new techniques, processes, and instruments. For the Australian colonies, one such experimental innovation was lithography.

Lithography flourished as a print form in part because of the colonial experimental mentality but also because the Australian colonies were free from the patent restrictions that existed in Europe. Prior to the *Paris Convention for the Protection of Industrial Property*,[43] patent owners had no claim to monopoly rights in the Australian colonies.[44] This is significant because by this time, a number of patents had been registered in Europe and elsewhere around the world for advances in lithography.

Many of these advances had been communicated to the colonies and were reported in the press. For example in 1838, English printer and publisher Charles Knight received a British patent for 'Improvements in the Process and in the Apparatus used in the Production of Coloured Impressions on Paper, Vellum, Parchment, and Pasteboard by Surface Printing'.[45] Knight called his colour printing process 'Illuminated Printing' – for the economical printing of coloured pictures, maps, and drawings.

In the following year, advances in mass printing and stereotyping were made by French printer Paul-François Dupont who was described as '[a] man-of the greatest talents in the arts …' who laid '… claim to priority in this discovery, as is always the case, when success has been obtained'.[46] The process, which he developed together with his brother Auguste was called 'Litho-Typographie' and was exhibited at the Paris Exhibition in 1839 with the promise of providing a quick and cheap way of making copies of printed works using stone printing. A series of other patents were also granted and noted in the local press, including for a lithographic printing press operated by steam,[47] a patent for 'The Antographie Press', which was registered to Waterlow and Son in England in 1851,[48] while patents were secured in France and England for a machine stone press.[49]

Lithography continued to flourish even after the Australian legislatures enacted general patent legislation, the first Act being passed in New South Wales in 1852 and later in Victoria in 1856.[50] This is because these same European inventors did not seek to register their printing patents in the Australian colonies with the same vigour as they had abroad.[51] Moreover, when patent legislation was introduced into the colonies, there was a healthy local disregard for patent rights and intellectual property more generally, as epitomised by the resistance to Osborne's claim to photolithography. The lack of local patent claims around the printing process and the general apathy towards

<
Charles Troedel Lithographer (c 1870)
Troedel Family Archive

intellectual property rights freed up the use of stone presses and new lithographic printing processes in Australia. It is no wonder the Australian Government was an enthusiastic and early adopter of lithography. This also explains why presses were being frequently imported and advertised for sale in great numbers in the newspaper classifieds, just a few years after the first presses were introduced into Australia.[52]

Lithography served the colonies well because it allowed colonial governments to promote a certain rhetoric which advanced its interest – promoting the natural beauty and possibility of life in the Australian colonies in order to attract free settlers and investment to Australia. This is certainly evident in some of the earliest commissioned lithographic prints. It was also plain from the language and imagery used in early colonial advertising and branding. Art, therefore, was used as a tool of coercion and lithography made that tool even more persuasive.

The first lithographic printing presses were brought to Australia in 1821 by the newly appointed Governor of New South Wales Sir Thomas Brisbane, not long after being introduced into the United States by Bass Otis in 1819. One of these presses was purchased by the Colonial Government, presumably as a means to control colonial communication. The other was used by Augustus Earle. Earle was the first professional artist to work in Australia.[53] Significantly, Earle's *Views in Australia* (1826) – consisting of five lithographs mounted in an album with a lithographed introduction and the bookplate of Sir Ralph Darling, the Governor of New South Wales from 1825 to 1831 – are considered to be the first printed lithographs in Australia.[54]

Developments in chemical printing in Australia moved rapidly following these initial forays into lithography, and were supported by the urgent need for large quantities of maps during the Victorian gold rush. It was this need that led to the purported invention of photolithography in Melbourne in 1859 by John Walter Osborne, which was reported as being used commercially in Australia by the Victorian Parliament in the same year.[55] Shortly after in 1865, the first chromolithographs were produced.[56] By 1889, a *Lithographic Artists and Engravers Club* was formed in Melbourne,[57] which had become a lithographic hub in

Australia. Indeed, Melbourne was home to several successful lithographic printers including Schuhkraffts, Macartney & Galbraith, as well as James J Blundell & Co and Campbell & Ferguson, both of whom printed many of the works by artist S T Gill.[58] Sydney also boasted a long list of lithographic printers including Allan & Wigley, Brown & Shaw, J B Benton and W J Robinson. And then there was Troedel & Co.

While the initial interest in and thirst for lithography stemmed from the government, the public soon developed an appetite for the prints too. Demand grew as the number of free settlers began to outnumber transported convicts and the masses started to buy printed lithographs to decorate their homes. At the same time, demand for commercial printing grew beyond serving the needs of the government.

The burgeoning market for lithographs and the success of lithographic printing businesses contributed to the local fascination with international advances in the technology, which were routinely reported in the daily newspapers.[59] Newspapers even included several notes on the history of '... the beautiful [a]rt of [l]ithography ...' and its 'accidental invention' by Senefelder.[60] The stunning result was that up until the first centenary of European settlement of Australia, all pictorial prints produced in the colonies were lithographs.[61] Front and centre of this burgeoning lithographic community was Charles Troedel.

Even though 'The Melbourne Album' is routinely cited as Troedel's foremost work, Troedel & Co were in no way limited to the production of scenic chromolithographs. Indeed, Troedel & Co endured because of its great success in commercial printing. Over the years, Troedel expanded to provide printing services for letterheads, business cards, corporate stationary, plans and personal stationary. The company was skilled in printing show cards, trade cards, posters including theatrical showbills, and labels of every description – for wine and spirit merchants, chemists, aerated water, cordial, biscuits and confectanary as well as collections for jams, preserved fruits, alcohol, soaps, candles, tea, coffee, tobacco, sauces and condiments.

Troedel also produced a series of larger advertising posters, which are remembered as having set a standard that has seldom been surpassed.[62] In fact, Troedel & Co were awarded the gold medal at the 1881 Melbourne International Exhibition, and in 1883 Troedel was awarded a silver medal at the Calcutta International Exhibition for specimens in lithography.[63]

These works are part of the collection that was donated to the State Library of Victoria in 1968, containing almost 10,000 print specimens.[64] Together, they represent '... the most significant printer's archive to survive in a public collection.'[65] They also provide a comprehensive dossier of Australia's advertising history, highlighting the dramatic shift in the styling of these works, which was only made possible by lithography and the skill and craftsmanship of Charles Troedel. These works span the domestic and public spheres, and as will be shown in the following chapters, chart a history of print advertising in colonial Australia – in the home, at the bar, in health and hygiene, in fashion and style and in leisurely pursuits.

II
In the Home

∧
R.H. & Co. New Season's
Teas For Sale Here.
Brisbane 1890–1891 (1890)
State Library Victoria,
H2000.180/114

As well as showcasing the pure artistry of his craft, the Troedel archive captures a significant shift in the Australian advertising aesthetic, away from the textual classified advertising that dominated early advertising practice since the publication of the first newspaper in 1803,[1] and towards a more graphical style. This transformation was most prominent in the home and its pantry stocks of packaged, processed and preserved food, and the spectacular prints Troedel produced for food wholesalers, importers and manufacturers.

In the Home

The change in advertising aesthetic partly stemmed from the growing competition for consumer goods and consumerism generally, which demanded more visual advertising beyond the pages of newspapers and magazines. Advances in food processing and packaging, which allowed producers to communicate directly to consumers in a way never before possible also contributed, allowing firms to permeate the private sphere and bring this new advertising culture into people's homes.

And then there was lithography. There is no doubt the palpable change in advertising style and design would not have been possible without lithography. The print process allowed for the production of inexpensive, high-quality illustrations for use as labels, as well as the reproduction of original paintings, drawings and sketches, which were used for full-page advertisements, advertising posters and trade cards.[2]

Chromolithography, which facilitated easy, high volume colour printing was even more instrumental, with advances in typography providing additional artistic choice for artists working in the medium. The advertising poster for *Yorick Bacon and Hams* (c 1881–1890), printed by Troedel & Co, is just one example of the production quality possible using lithography. In this example, the graduated tonal background is dramatically punctuated by the violent blood red ink used for the leading text, and to brand the featured animals with their fate.

Historically, most food was sold and packaged using paper, cloth, wooden crates and glass. These materials were limited in their storage and preservation properties. They also necessarily limited the way such goods could be visually presented. In the 1800s, new discoveries and manufacturing developments based on the science of food safety and preservation led to a change in the nature of food packaging. By default, this also led to a change in product labelling and advertising practice.[3]

Packaging creates a dialogue between consumers and producers, and so these new packing methods were central to the broader history of advertising and branding, as they were an important marketing tool for producers. Before the era of wide aisle supermarkets, self-service and orderly open-access shelving, consumer goods were located on shelves behind a counter and retrieved by a store clerk upon request. These sale conditions presented the need for visually arresting packaging that consumers could see and identify from a distance across the shop counter. The sale of food in tins and canisters and the introduction of canned food enabled this, allowing for the addition of distinctive paper labels which provided a ready-made advertising canvas that producers had never before had at their disposal.[4]

Developments in paper manufacturing meant that these types of paper labels became the most common method for labelling pre-packaged foods, compared with previous practice, where metal cans and tins were typically embossed and inscribed with descriptive words and designs.[5] The nineteenth century was a pivotal period in this respect, with the onset of the mass production of paper bags and paperboard carton.[6] These developments can be traced back to the invention of the paper-making machine in 1798 by Frenchman Nicolas-Louis Robert, which led to the production of paperboard by John Dickinson in Hertfordshire.[7]

It was inevitable that lithographers would take advantage of these changes and ultimately come to dominate the print label trade.[8] It resulted in booming business abroad. The London print directories listed 700 lithographers by 1854, while 700 printers were listed in the United States in 1887.[9] Eventually, print prices increased along with demand. *The New York Sun* reported in 1888 that the average cost for 1,000 labels had increased from $10 to $50.[10] The increased prices were matched by an increase in quality, with the same report noting that while '… a few years ago any kind of label was considered good enough to put on a cigar box …' now '[t]he label is often better than the cigar.'[11] A similar trend emerged in the Australian colonies, with Charles Troedel amassing a substantial share of the local paper print market, where he produced high quality, award-winning work, which was recognised on the national and international stage.

Yorick BACON

SPECIAL MILD

AND

CURED ON THE ENGLISH SYSTEM

The BREAKFAST DELICACY

TROEDEL & Cº
LITH. MELB

A New Advertising Canvas

The invention of the metal can and new methods in canned food preservation were perhaps the most critical factor in shifting established practice in the packaging of and advertising for, food for the home.[12] The metal can was invented in 1809 after General Napoleon Bonaparte made an offer of 12,000 francs for anyone who could invent a cheap and effective method to preserve food. The cash award was prompted by the need to supply his growing army with regular supplies of quality food. It was also motivated by a desire to extend military campaigns into the summer and autumn months, which had not been possible because of the limited availability of food.

Frenchman Nicolas Appert was awarded the prize in 1810, after inventing a method of sealing food in tin airtight cans and sterilising them through a boiling process.[13] He wrote about the method in the same year in *L'Art de Conserver les Substances Animales et Végétales*, which was translated and later published in English as *The Art of Preserving All Kinds of Animal and Vegetable Substances for Several Years*.[14] Despite winning a gold medal from the Société d'Encouragement pour l'Industrie Nationale (the Society for the Encouragement of National Industry), and receiving critical acclaim for his discovery, the reasons for the lack of spoilage were unknown to Appert at the time. It would be another 50 years before Louis Pasteur provided the answer, having identified the role of microbes in food spoilage, in his most recognised career achievement.

Appert's method for food preservation was quickly adopted around the world, initially by the military, but it also came to serve the broader population. By the middle of the nineteenth century, canned food became something of a status symbol amongst middle-class households. Canned foods were also favoured by the early explorers because of its stability and beginning in 1814, canned foods were sent to the British colonies, including Australia.[15] In fact, tin cans reached Australia for the first time in 1815 and were an essential tool in freeing the colonies from its dependence on British food producers.[16]

It took a few decades for local efforts in canned food production to surface. The first person to can food in Australia was Sizar Elliott. Elliott opened a small canning factory in Sydney in 1846, with the intention of developing a canned export trade to take advantage of the oversupply of local livestock. He was noted for being the first person to display Australian tinned meat at an exhibition in Sydney, and was awarded a medallion 20 years later after exhibiting his tins again to demonstrate how well the product had been preserved.[17] Although he failed commercially, Elliott's efforts paved the way for others who were more successful.[18] By 1869, several manufacturers in Queensland had emerged, who together were exporting over one million kilograms of canned meat each year.[19]

Locally grown fruit and vegetables were also canned and preserved in abundance during the 1800s and into the twentieth century. Fruit and vegetables were preserved in pieces ready to eat. Much of the fruit was also used for canned jams and preserves. These canning businesses began to appear from around the 1870s, and were dotted all over Australia but especially in Victoria and Tasmania. Tasmania was particularly known for its quality produce. *The Tasmanian News* boasted about the colony's international reputation, observing how 'Tasmania is famous all over the world for its apples and is famous all over the Commonwealth for its jam.'[20] *The Mercury* put this reputation down to the Tasmanian soil and climate which '... contribute to make our fruit much more juicy, and to give them a more luscious flavour ...' than those grown on any part of the mainland.[21]

Many of these canning businesses were customers of Troedel & Co. Some of Troedel's most distinctive labels were used for canned fruits and jams, spanning into the twentieth century, and later extending to include an impressive array of labels which were affixed to wooden fruit crates. These paper labels were hand-glued onto tins by factory

<
Yorick Bacon and Hams (c 1881–1890)
State Library Victoria,
H2008.94/46

workers and splashed with bright colours and dramatic fonts. They were typically nestled with life-like depictions of fresh fruit and often featured orchards of apple and pear trees, and orange groves – bringing the Australian farming landscape into the city. These labels also became the talking point among traders and were displayed at the world exhibitions.

In Tasmania, the most successful producer of canned fruit was the Henry Jones Co. Henry Jones was born in 1862 and began his working life at age 12 in 1874 in George Peacock's Jam Factory in Hobart. His parents were convicts who were sent to Australia to serve their sentence separately, although they married sometime later. Working six days a week, ten hours a day, Jones pasted labels on jam tins during his time at Peacock's. At the age of 27, Jones purchased a share of the factory and in 1895, George Peacock transferred all his jam-making interests to Jones. In the same year, Jones expanded his canning empire and purchased the Jam Factory in Melbourne. It was during this period that Jones established the renowned IXL brand, derived from his personal motto – 'I excel in everything I do' – which was used in the firm's advertising thereafter.[22]

Peacock's Jam Factory was one of the first businesses to can jams in Australia and the firm's founder, George Peacock, was '… regarded as one of the pioneers of the fruit-preserving industry in Tasmania, if not in the Australian colonies'.[23] The company manufactured its own cans using imported Welsh tinplate, with each can hand-soldered and hand-washed before filling. This production process was no small task, with reports of young girls scouring rust from the tin sheets, which had been damaged by salt water en route to Australia.[24] The firm also produced the boxes used for packing produce, which were made of wood from the northern rivers of Tasmania.[25]

Troedel printed material for both Henry Jones and George Peacock, whose unique and sophisticated designs were described as '… having a good harmony of colour about it [which] attracted attention'.[26] The advertising poster titled *I Come Full Speed to Tell You Peacock's Jams & Jellies Cannot be Excelled* (c 1881-1890) is similarly eye-catching. The garish poster for Peacock's assortment of fruit jams and jellies depicts a naked screaming child sitting atop a steam train. The 14.5 x 9.7 centimetre poster was produced between 1881 and 1890 in muted blue and grey tones, which adds to the macabre feel of the poster. It also hints

to the IXL motto – with the statement 'I Come Full Speed to Tell You Peacock's Jams & Jellies Cannot be Excelled' emblazoned across the front of the train and the poster.

As with many of the labels and posters produced for tinned fruits and jams, the labels presented here have a depth and richness of colour. The labels also demonstrate the growing experimentation with new font styles, with as much prominence placed on the fonts as an artistic form as the illustrations themselves. Printers like Troedel & Co took advantage of developments in typography and the introduction of serif typefaces, which were developed in the late eighteenth and early nineteenth century and were a radical break from the traditional typography of the time with its high contrast of strokes, straight serifs and a vertical axis in the style of Bodoni and others.[27] These experimental designs also featured on the tins and canisters popularly used to store and sell biscuits, coffee and tea, which were routinely adorned with paper labels produced by the growing number of Australian lithographers, including Troedel & Co.

>

I Come Full Speed to Tell You Peacock's Jams & Jellies Cannot be Excelled (c 1881-1890)
State Library Victoria,
H2008.94/20

EMPIRE COMPY'S

TRADE MARK

DANDELION

COCOA

Agents, Robert Harper & Co.

MELBOURNE SYDNEY ADELAIDE BRISBANE

R. HARPER & Co's NEW LABEL

REGISTERED as TRADE MARK

Harper & Co's ORIENTAL

COFFEE

MELBOURNE AND SYDNEY

R. HARPER & Co's

PEARL

RICE

EMPIRE COMPY'S

TRADE MARK

DANDELION

COFFEE

Agents, Robert Harper & Co.

MELBOURNE SYDNEY ADELAIDE BRISBANE

Robert Harper & Co's Assorted Labels (c 1880)
State Library Victoria, Miscellaneous

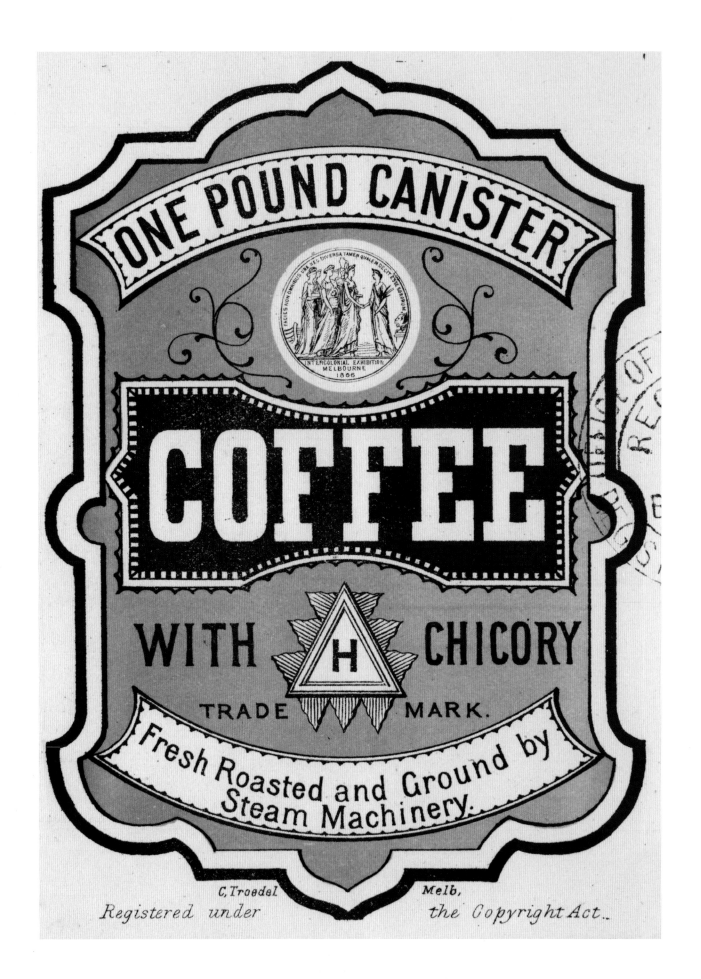

Labels of Archaeological Record

In addition to the benefits of easy transportation and preserved freshness, the great utility of canning and the use of tins and canisters for the sale and storage of pantry staples was the addition of pictorial designs, which were used to convey information about their contents. Interestingly, descriptive pictorial representations of goods in this way was one of the last kinds of illustrations to appear on food packaging.[28] Instead, symbols, decorative text, and the arms of trade guilds or associations were commonly used. Landscapes and illustrations of a firm's warehouse or factory site were also commonly featured. Biscuit manufacturers were especially known for this. Huntley & Palmer for example, who became biscuit makers to the British Royal Family, used factory views on many of their biscuit tins, serving as an archaeological record of the industrial development of the firm, marking its progress and expansion over time.[29] Troedel & Co also incorporated factory designs on its biscuit labels.

Troedel's catalogue includes prints for the first biscuit company in Australia, Swallow & Ariell.[30] Another biscuit manufacturer included in the archive is Thomas Bibby Guest. Guest was born in England in 1830 and arrived in Sydney in 1852 with his father. Together, they began making biscuits under the name TB Guest & Co at a small factory on Pitt Street. A few years later, the Sydney factory was closed and, following a three-and-a-half month journey on a bullock wagon packed with his plant and machinery, Guest arrived in Melbourne.[31]

By May 1856, Guest had established a steam biscuit factory in Melbourne in partnership with John Barnes. Trading as Barnes, Guest & Co, the firm took out a five-year lease on a building in William Street. In 1858, the firm reorganised as T B Guest & Co. A new store was built at the William Street site in 1869, where they remained until 1932 when the business moved to West Melbourne. In 1963, a merger with another biscuit manufacturer created Arnott Guest Pty Ltd, and the origins of one of Australia's most iconic biscuit brands was established.

In *T. B. Guest & Co. Steam Biscuit Factory, William Street Melbourne* (1878), the Guest Factory is the central focus, with the red brick building and yellow stone dressings standing prominently. In front of the building is a horse and carriage, and another two horse-drawn delivery carts sits to the side of each other. A gentleman, possibly Guest, is standing by the front door decked in a frock coat and top hat. The illustrations Troedel printed for Guest placed the abovementioned William Street factory as the focal point, surrounded by experimental fonts. They were also decorated with the firm's many medals. *T. B. Guest & Co. Steam Biscuit Factory, William Street Melbourne* (c 1870-1879) stands out for its nod to Victorian era styling, with the poster heavily segmented with ornamental borders including the classic elements of layering, sampling of pen flourishes with geometric traceries and interwoven patterns. It includes an aerial view of the biscuit factory and was scattered with sprouting flowers and vines, hinting to the art nouveau styling of the early twentieth century.

Tea, coffee and other shelf-stable groceries were also commonly packaged in metal tins and canisters and draped with decorative paper labels. Troedel's archive includes whole albums dedicated to labels used for tea leaves and coffee canisters. As for the trove of tea labels, this is not surprising since tea was consumed excessively throughout colonial Australia. By the late nineteenth century, this fact was '... to be deplored, for when taken in excess it causes severe functional derangement of the digestive organs, and prejudicially affects the nervous system'.[32] Although most of the tea consumed in Australia was grown and produced overseas, there were a number of local merchants who purchased leaves from China and India and packaged them to sell under their own labels and brands. Many of these were clients of Troedel & Co.

These labels routinely referenced the Chinese and Indian connection to tea. China and India have long feuded over who can claim to be the birthplace of tea, with both origins reflected in the way tea leaves were labelled and advertised. In China, tea

<

One Pound Canister Coffee (1871)
State Library Victoria,
H96.160/2100

T.B. GUES

ESTABLISHED 1856.

BISCUIT   GUEST'S

Steam Biscu

William Street N

Richard Wendel (1851-1926),
*T. B. Guest & Co. Steam Biscuit Factory,
William Street Melbourne* (1878)
State Library Victoria,
H2000.180/195

T. B. Guest & Co. Steam Biscuit Factory,
William Street Melbourne (c 1870-1879)
State Library Victoria,
H2000.180/200

was traditionally prepared by steaming tea leaves, pounding them in a mortar, then pressing them into cakes to be baked dry. Those cakes were subsequently ground to a powder in a mortar, then boiled with water and a pinch of salt in an iron pot and poured into bowls. This traditional method was alluded to in the way tea was marketed, and it was usual to see iron teapots and bowls depicted on labels for Chinese leaf tea.

During the nineteenth century, Chinese tea labels also frequently featured bright colouring and bold designs, and were sometimes printed on thin rice paper. This was true of the labels produced by Troedel & Co too. Many of the packages printed for local tea merchants also featured intricate woodblock printing patterns, which were typically used throughout East Asia as a method of printing on textiles and paper. These patterns were traditionally hand painted using multiple colours, sometimes with a gold foil effect. *Licensed Victuallers Two Star Tea Association* (1876) is one example of a tea wrapper featuring the woodblock print, combined with the Victorian style borders to bring the East and West together in the washed-out purple print.

One of Troedel's main customers whose tea labels featured prominently in the archive was the colonial wholesaler and manufacturing grocer Robert Harper & Co Limited.[33] The label *New Season's Teas 1891-92* (1891) is a particularly

arresting example. This label was printed in the shape of a fan and was textured with shadowed layers to create a dramatic three-dimensional concertina effect. It also featured two workers in traditional dress, pulling a copper pot of new season Indian, Chinese and Ceylon teas. A woman standing in the centre appears to be directing the two men and the teapot cart, while wielding a parasol.

Established in Melbourne in 1865 by colonial businessman and politician Robert Harper, the company initially traded in tea, coffee and spices from the East Indies before expanding and later manufacturing a range of awarding winning products. By the middle of the 1870s, Harper was a leading Melbourne merchant, later establishing branches in Sydney (1877), Adelaide (1882), Brisbane (1887) and later in the other colonies including New Zealand.[34]

Robert Harper & Co Limited was known for their sophisticated packaging and design. After showing at the Queensland International Exhibition in Brisbane in 1897, there was '[m]arked interest ... shown by the public in the very attractive exhibit of Messers Robert Harper and Co ...'.[35] By this time, the company was well recognised for their established lines for starch, cocoa, coffee, essence, oatmeal, rolled oats, baking powder, self-raising flour, table jellies, curry powder, patent groats, patent barley, culinary essences, blended teas, cocoa and coffee.

The Tea of the Times (1888)
State Library Victoria,
H2000.180/109

The Hindoo Blend Pure Tea (c 1880-1890)
State Library Victoria,
H2000.180/110

The company was perhaps best known for their coffee and the beautifully decorated canisters they were presented in, as designed and printed by Troedel & Co. This included an extensive range of roasts and blends, which were advertised under different brands, and had earnt the trust and respect of the consuming public. *The Queenslander* reported that: '[o]f their familiar brand of coffee and chicory the foremost is the Empire Company's Oriental brand … while the Zouave and Imperial French brands … are very attractive. Robert Harper and Co.'s name has been associated with that of coffee in the minds of people for a considerable number of years past, and this is a further guarantee, if any is required, of the excellence of their manufactures in this direction.'[36]

The label *One Pound Canister Coffee* (1871) was one of a series of similar labels printed by Troedel for the firm. This 12 x 8.6 centimetre label was printed in black and white against a soft blue-green background for its chicory roast and included an illustration of the firm's medal from the Intercolonial Exhibition in Melbourne in 1866, with an H featured inside a triangle, referencing the firm's founder. The label, like most of the firm's labels, was registered for copyright protection in Victoria, highlighting the value the company placed on its branding efforts, and how much these labels ultimately added to their financial success.

Hidden beneath these iconic labels and brilliant designs was a counter-narrative about colonialism and race. It is no secret that advertising was used historically to foster and build national identities. The ads shown here, and within the broader Troedel archive, were being used to sell more than just a product. The ads were being used for a bigger sell – to sell Australia as a white, civilised part of the British Empire. This meant capitalising on the fruits of that colonial empire, an empire built on the backs of others. And capitalising on the portrayal of 'the others'.

This reality and the intimate connection between tea, coffee and empire has attracted a great deal of attention in academic circles, with this scholarship exploring how these products were used throughout history to shape and perpetuate the British Empire.[37] This narrative is referenced in the label for *New Season's Teas* 1891-1892 (1891), where the men hauling the copper teapot on their backs look to be under great stress, working under laborious or slave like conditions. It is also evident in the branding used by some firms, such as the EMPIRE branded tea and coffee in *Robert Harper & Co's Assorted Labels* (c 1880). The portrayal of the otherness is painfully apparent in brands like *The Hindoo Blend Pure Tea* (c 1880-1890), *The Oriental Tea Company Packet Tea* (c 1880-1890), which was drawn by respected artist and illustrator Charles Turner and *The Tea of the Times* (1888).

New Season's Teas 1891-1892 (c 1891)
State Library Victoria, Miscellaneous

CTROEDEL & Cº LITH. MELB.& SYD.

Charles Turner (active 1869-1900),
*The Oriental Tea Company
Packet Tea* (c 1881-1890)
State Library Victoria,
H2000.212/10

*Licensed Victuallers Two
Star Tea Association* (1876)
State Library Victoria,
H96.160/2408

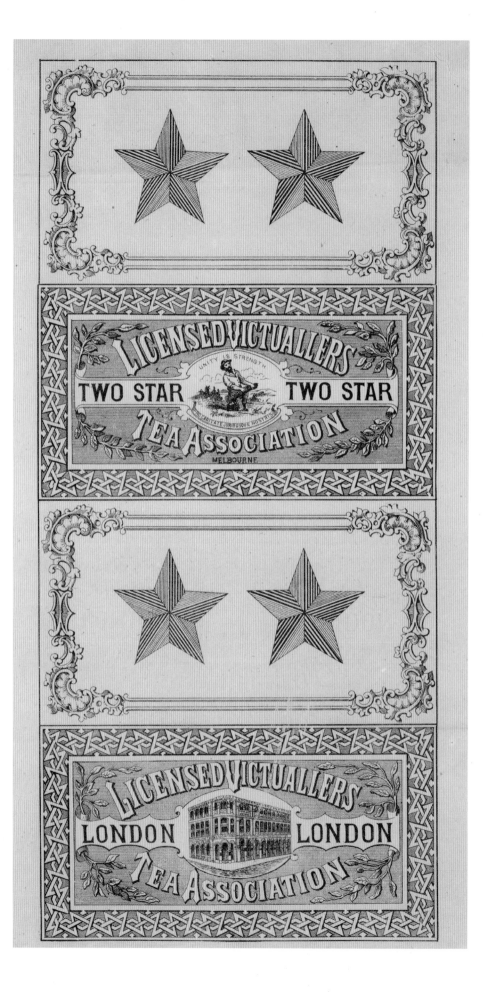

Artistic Form and Commercial Function

There was an obvious appeal for traders to use labels on cans, tins and canisters as a means of attracting custom. The firms who commissioned Troedel to produce these labels understood they carried significant commercial value. As such, they sought to protect these designs, submitting hundreds of applications for copyright registration. The labels for *Superior Raspberry Vinegar* (1872), which was registered in 1872, is just the tip of the iceberg.

The practice of registering advertising material for copyright protection was widespread in the Australian colonies. In Victoria, Troedel's prints cluttered the copyright register, even though many of these works, but particularly product labels were largely descriptive, and not at all similar to the kinds of original creative works normally associated with copyright protection, and artistic works in particular. This mimicked a similar trend that had emerged overseas including in the United States and United Kingdom, where the international copyright registers were littered with lithographs.[38] So, while the practice of registering portrait and artistic lithographs was largely uncontroversial, lithographs printed for advertising purposes, such as labels, raised a unique series of concerns.

These concerns came to a head in the United States in the decision *Scoville v Toland*, a case involving the reproduction of a medicine label for 'Doctor Rodgers' Compound Syrup of Liverwort and Tar', which had been registered for copyright protection.[39] Here, the Court rejected the plaintiff's claim, holding the labels served a purely commercial purpose of identifying goods for sale and therefore could not be protected as copyright works.

In doing so, Justice McClean distinguished labels from lunar tables (which set out the dates of the various phases of the moon and are purely factual), sonata, music and other mental labours, which could attract copyright protection. The distinction was made on the basis that these mental labours made a lasting contribution to learning through knowledge dissemination instead of being ephemeral or commercial in character. Labels, such as the medicine labels in the case '... are only valuable when connected with the medicine. As labels they are useful, but as mere compositions, distinct from the medicine, they are never used or designed to be used.'[40]

Based on this reasoning, a label, no matter how artful, could not be registered for copyright protection. Notwithstanding this decision, the distinction between the various categories of lithographs was not always applied in practice, as evidenced by the thousands of registered labels across the continents. Eventually, the registration of these kinds of works was validated by the United States Supreme Court in *George Bleistein v Donaldson Lithographing Company*, which held that advertisements for a circus were copyrightable subject matter, with Justice Holmes noting '... [a] picture is nonetheless a picture, and nonetheless a subject of copyright, that it is used for an advertisement.'[41]

The registration of advertising prints attracted the same kind of criticism locally. In fact, some believed that had it not been for the habit of registering these advertisements and labels for copyright protection in Victoria, the necessity of legislation permitting trade mark registration would have arisen sooner than 1876 when the *Trade Marks Registration Act 1876* (Vic) was enacted. On this, it was observed in 1882 that '[t]he [l]aw of [c]opyright was never intended to protect trade labels, but this practice was presumably allowed in earlier years because there was then no proper legislative machinery for the registration of Trade Marks in existence ...'[42]

This was evident from the limited protection afforded to trade material by the copyright system. So, while copyright registration did serve as notice to other traders that a claim had been made over a work, in the case of infringement, the owner was only entitled to an award of damages for copying. Moreover, a copyright owner was not eligible for damages for trade diversion or lost sales caused by consumer confusion. Copyright law therefore only gave rise to the right against copying. It did not give authors the exclusive right to use those works in the course of trade.

Trade mark registration overcame these limitations and provided a range of protection for brands and commercial reputation that copyright did not. Persistent lobbying by traders in the Australian colonies and in Britain resulting in the enactment of the *Merchandise Marks Act 1862* (UK) and the *Trade Marks Registration Act 1875* (UK), led to the eventual enactment of trade mark legislation facilitating trade mark registration from the 1860s up until the 1880s in Australia.[43] There were several motivations behind the introduction of trade mark legislation and registration.[44] Lithography was also part of the complex matrix.

Stone press printing made the reproduction of trade marks and advertising materials easier than ever before, and so facilitated the production of counterfeits and imitations. Lithography also made it possible to produce trade marks that were commercially valuable and worth protecting. As such, when lithography reached its peak and became the printing means of choice in the Australian colonies in the 1870s and 1880s, it resulted in an influx of applications for labels as trade marks, including those printed by Troedel.

Many of these labels, which became increasingly ornate and used of dozens of bright and often gaudy colours, were primitive in their attempt to distinguish, and were mostly descriptive of the products to which they were affixed, and lacking in features that would serve to differentiate between brands or traders. These developments coincided with the advent of trade cards displayed on shop counters. Special edition trade cards were fiercely sought after, and the advertising function of these cards quickly diminished, replaced by their aesthetic value as collectables.

These stylistic choices were openly frowned upon, with the bureaucracy commenting that '[a] label is not unfrequently registered which contains a whole sermon, treatise, or history, and without any distinctive mark at all, other than, perhaps, the border of the label'.[45] There was a slow, growing disdain for the practice, as acknowledged in a report on The Patents and Copyrights Office of Melbourne, which included a report on the Trade Marks' Office. The report described the trade-marking of labels as '... ultra vires altogether of the meaning of a trade mark, and of the spirit of the trade mark laws'.[46] That is because '... a "trade mark" should in no sense be a treatise, and that the interpretation of the word "label" cannot in any way be strained to embrace so unnecessary a meaning.'[47] Indeed the courts had long been wary of framing a trade mark in this broad way, including Lord Westbury in the seminal 1865 decision of *Leather Cloth Co v American Leather Cloth*, who observed that '... what is here called by the Appellants a trade mark, is, in reality, an advertisement of the character and quality of their marks.'[48]

Even so, these works continued to be registered thanks to the broad definition of a trade mark which included the word 'labels'.[49] The lack of case law providing clarity on the matter contributed to the continuing practice.[50] This objectionable practice did diminish and was said to be in decline in Victoria by 1879, after it was reportedly discouraged by British trade mark officials.[51] At the same time, the underlying artistic works still qualified for copyright protection with this controversy resolving itself in Australia in the same way the issue was resolved in the United States in *George Bleistein v Donaldson Lithographing Company*.[52]

And over time, the definition of a trade mark was interpreted more strictly to protect distinctive signs, to the exclusion of purely descriptive matter featured on labels, where those labels lacked any other distinctive indicia.[53] But this maturation of the intellectual property system was only following a decades long process, which eventually carved out a more defined delineation between copyright and trade mark law – a delineation that was brought to bear by developments in lithography – and the proliferation of Troedel & Co's lithographs.[54]

Superior Raspberry Vinegar (1872)
State Library Victoria,
H96.160/2136

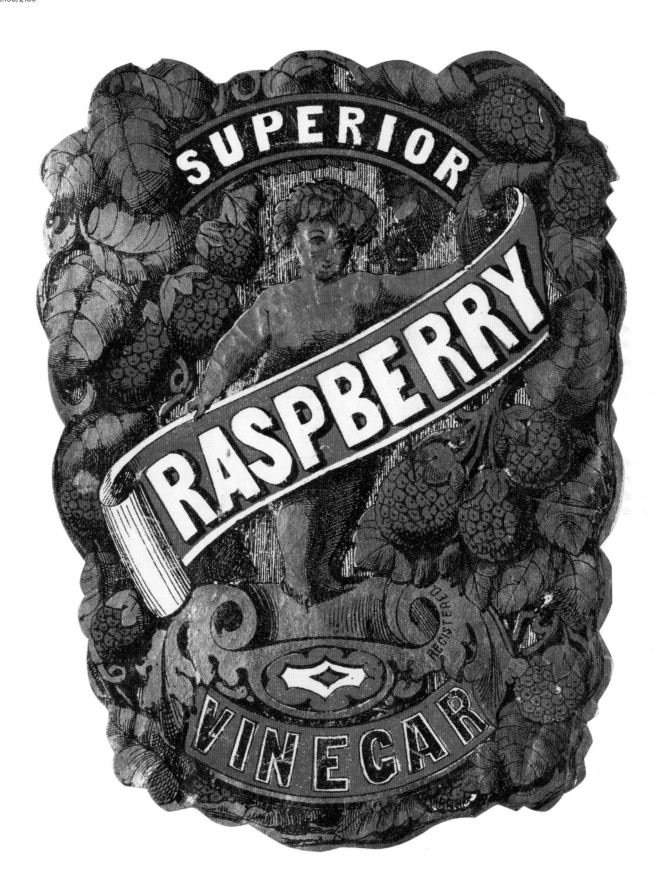

III
At the Bar

The

CELEBRATED

TRADE LION MARK

CAMERONS

RED TAG
TOBACCO

SOLD HERE

TROEDEL & Cº MELB.

^
*The Celebrated Red
Tag Tobacco Camerons*
(c 1881-1890)
State Library Victoria,
H2008.94.90

Excessive alcohol consumption developed early in Australia and played a central part in colonial social life.[1] Many historians have attested to this.

Three Men Drinking and Smoking (c 1880-1900)
State Library Victoria,
H2000.180/151

In describing the first colonists, for example, Russel Ward wrote that '... no people on the face of the earth absorbed more alcohol per head of population.'[2] Some even described the early colonists as being '... steeped in alcohol'.[3] According to early estimates, an average of 13.6 litres of alcohol was consumed by New South Wales inhabitants in the 1830s.[4] Subsequent historical accounts have since challenged claims that Australian consumption rates were the highest in the world.[5] Nevertheless, the historical legend remains, thanks to popular literature and folklore of the time.

In 1869, the satirical journal *Humbug* featured Marcus Clarke's essay *The Curse of the Country*, where he wrote of a nation of drunkards where '[n]o man can hope to succeed in business, profession, or society, unless he is prepared to take his chance of death in an asylum for inebriates.'[6] Similar themes featured in Henry Kendall's poem *The Demon of Drink*.[7] These accusations were echoed by government, with Colonel David Collins observing in 1793 that: 'The passion for liquor was so predominant among the people that it operated like a mania, there being nothing that they would not risk to obtain it, and while spirits were to be had, those who did any extra labour refused to be paid in money or in any other article than spirits.'[8]

The Troedel collection provides a graphical representation of the ingrained and entrenched cultural custom of drinking in Australia during the nineteenth century. It started with rum before tastes and technology shifted to beer and a thriving brewing industry. During this period, drinking became a glamorised and normalised part of everyday life. It was even associated with royalty, as shown in *The Prince of Wales Finest Old Scotch Blend Whisky* (c 1881-1890) where a portrait of Prince Albert is used to sell Old Scotch Whisky.

Drinking was a civilised pastime, as was smoking. This is shown in *Three Men Drinking and Smoking* (c 1880-1900). In this illustration, three men sit around the table in a drawing room, laughing and recounting the day's events, still wearing their riding gear. The men are surrounded by a bottle of spirits, full glasses and a box of cigars – their faces brimming with merriment. The subjects are well dressed, wearing jackets that look to be made of silk and velvet, alluding to their status and wealth. Two weary dogs sit at the feet of the table, by the fireplace, exhausted after the day's events.

Consumption was more than just a way to pass time. Alcohol was also used as a legitimate currency to reward hard labour. That is not to mention the perceived medicinal benefits of alcohol, and the therapeutic uses to which it was put – stimulating and supporting the system, preventing fevers and infectious diseases and providing the stamina for the manual workforce.[9] Furthermore, in Europe, alcohol had long served as a source of nutrition, as the diets of the time were restricted and the choice was limited – a trend that continued in Australia.

By the turn of the century however, the temperance movement grew in momentum and advocated against consumption, criticising alcohol intoxication and promoting abstinence. While the local movement, led by American Jessie A Ackermann and the Woman's Christian Temperance Union, failed to bring prohibition to Australia as it had in the United States, it did have a discernible impact. The result was a surge in saccharine non-alcoholic beverages, and advertising ephemera to match.

The Prince of Wales Finest
Old Scotch Blend Whisky
(c 1881-1890)
State Library Victoria,
H2008.94/81

*Finest Standard Old Vintage
Brandy Cognac* (c 1871)
State Library Victoria,
H96.160/2124

The Rum State and Rebellion

Australia's drinking culture began with the arrival of the First Fleet. Convicts and the colonists alike brought with them an ingrained habit of drinking to Australian shores. Alcohol was used to alleviate the trials of early settlement, the harshness of penal life and the isolation many felt being so far from home.[10] The introduction of alcohol to the Australian colonies began on the First Fleet, when Governor Phillip purchased rum and wine at Rio de Janiero en route. The fleet bought 65,000 litres of rum for the remainder of the voyage, and for the first three years of the colony. Rum supplies were distributed among the marines and their wives, while the wine was used in the hospital.[11] Even the convicts received a special issue of rum, notwithstanding that no provision had been made for them. As so the thirst for rum began.

Spirits remained in short supply until 1792 when the Imperial authorities sent another consignment. At the same time, private consignments arrived to meet growing demand. The consumption of spirits continued into the twentieth century, but wine and imported beer were consumed in large quantities.[12] Drinking games, such as 'shouting' and 'work and bust' only added to the culture of heavy drinking. These games involved a prolonged drinking spree following an extended period of hard work in the bush, a precursor to the modern-day binge drinking epidemic. The drinking culture was compounded by the fact that spirits were used to barter, and many convicts were paid in rum.

Rum is a central part of Australia's history, from the custom of rum as currency leading to the Rum State moniker,[13] to the Rum Rebellion in New South Wales in 1808 when Governor William Bligh was arrested and the colony was placed under military rule for the first and only time in history.[14] The Rum Rebellion is one of the greatest stories from Australia's convict history, with several revisionist accounts emerging over the years challenging the previous account of events.[15] Some economic historians have even gone so far as to say that New South Wales was not a colony awash in rum. Rather, the local inhabitants were more moderate than their British counterparts and that trade in spirits was not necessarily an extremely lucrative activity.[16]

The traditional account starts from the moment the New South Wales Corps – the Red Coats – were employed for military duties in the British penal colony and insisted on accumulating as much rum as possible. They even threatened to delay the sailing of the First Fleet if they were not allowed extra rations of rum on the voyage and for their service in the colony.[17] Once entrenched in the colony, the Corps sent ships to the nearest suppliers and imported rum back to Australia to drink, trade and sell at exorbitant profits. They also used the rum to buy favours. Successive governors tried to stop the Rum Corps, but to no avail. In time, their tactics led them to be known as 'the Rum Corps'.

Under the command of Major George Johnston, working closely with John Macarthur, the Rum Corps mounted the Rum Rebellion, deposing Governor Bligh on 26 January 1808, 20 years to the day after Arthur Phillip founded the first European settlement in Australia. For several years before the rebellion, Johnston claimed Bligh was abusive and interfering with the troops of the Rum Corps. During this period, Bligh had stopped Macarthur from cheaply distributing large quantities of rum into the Corps. He also halted Macarthur's allegedly illegal importation of stills equipment.

Tensions simmered, and when Macarthur failed to appear in court for his failure to make good on a bond, and ended up in jail on the order of Bligh, the rebellion was in full motion. Johnston issued an order to release Macarthur. Upon his release, Macarthur drafted a petition for Johnston to arrest Bligh and take charge of the colony. With this, the Rum Corps marched to Government House to arrest Bligh – and the rest is history.[18]

The historical significance of rum is evident in Troedel's catalogue and the collection of labels

<

Superior Jamaica Rum (c 1851–1885)
State Library Victoria,
H32088/12

for rum, most of which were for Jamaican Rum, including *Superior Jamaica Rum* (c 1851-1885), which features a picture of a pineapple with the words Jamaica Rum wrapped around it. The pineapple is brushed in gold – emphasising the plump, sweet fruit while also signalling rum's precious value as a colonial commodity. The label is trimmed with a decorative gold border with red accents, and is set against a green background.

Jamaican Rum was highly prized. By the middle of the eighteenth century, Jamaica was considered the premier English sugar colony. The average plantation was more than one hundred acres and exploited by slaves whose daily cultivation quota was one hundred cane holes.[19] In the early days, most rum was imported from the West Indies and, more commonly, from India. Rum was made from molasses, a by-product of sugar refining. In India, the raw product was often derived from palm sugar and not cane sugar, or a mix of both, resulting in poor quality product. Even so, while beer had been the favoured drink on British naval vessels early on, the colonial capture of sugar plantations in the West Indies in the seventeenth century made rum cheaper and more available. The tastes and drinking habits on-board adjusted accordingly.

Troedel's elaborately decorated labels for rum, with lashings of gold, company crests, monograms and decorative borders mostly camouflage the chequered history behind this beverage and how Imperial powers forcefully displaced west African peoples to cultivate sugar using slave labour.[20] One exception is *Old Jamaica Rum* (c 1875), which tells this story and the consequences of the sugar revolution in the space of a 7.5 x 12 centimetre label.

In this narrative drawing, the British naval explorer is standing next to a barrel of rum, charging his glass in the air as if he is about to make a toast. To his right, and the left of the image is a local tribesperson, wearing traditional head-dress and attire. He is standing in a defensive pose towards the British officer, leaning on a hand-crafted weapon. This pose may have been one of fear or resistance – but either way, it makes sense in the broader political context in which the pair meet. Indigenous populations began dying at unprecedented rates due to the influx of old world diseases brought by colonists during this period.[21] Estimates of these population losses vary from 8.4 million to 112.5 million.[22] In the background is

a naval vessel – docked, and ready to take the spoils back home.

This label taps into the broader narrative about how the British Empire harnessed the world's edible resources – from sugar, to pepper, tea, rice, cod and more – to define the world's food palate.[23] But it came at a cost, as the British pursued this mission without regard for local indigenous populations, or their land. There are clear parallels in the way the colonised are being depicted in the label *Old Jamaica Rum* (c 1875), and the labels used for tea tins and canisters, as canvassed in the previous chapter. In fact, there is no escaping the colonial brutality behind the Empire's unwavering quest for world domination, with this troubled history hidden in every corner of the Troedel archive.

Finest Jamaica Rum (c 1875)
State Library Victoria,
H96.160/2274

Old Jamaica Rum (c 1875)
State Library Victoria,
H96.160/2436

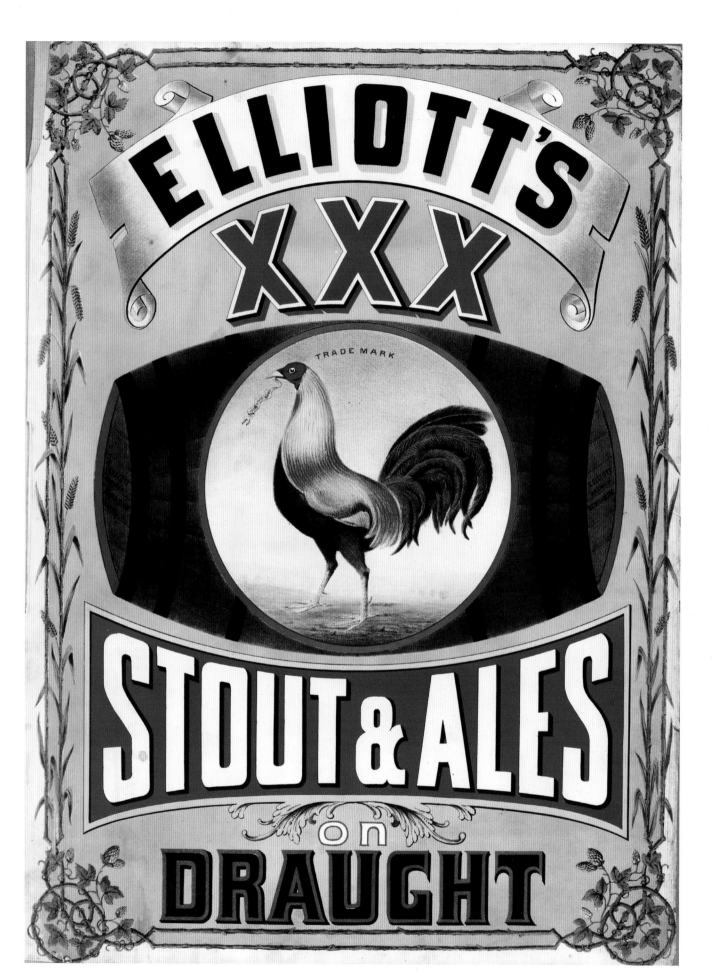

Brewing Boom

Although spirits, particularly rum were widely consumed in the early years of settlement, preferences changed as the century wore on, and tastes turned to beer. Like rum, beer has a long history in Australia, dating back to Captain James Cook's first charting of the East Coast of Australia in 1770, where Cook brewed beer to sterilise the ship's drinking water.

At the time, beer was seen as a healthier alternative to potent spirits like rum. John Boston set up the first official beer brewery in Australia in 1796, although there were convicts brewing beer illegally before him. Here, Boston made beer from Indian corn using the leaves of the cape gooseberry for bitters. His venture was so successful that within months, Boston had erected at some expense a building proper for the business, was granted 170 acres at Mulgrave Place, and had built a windmill.[24]

Melbourne's first supplies of beer were imported from Launceston by John Pascoe Fawkner. Locally, John Mills produced '… every palatable ale …' at his Flinders Street brewery.[25] Other early brewers included Thomas Capel at his Britannia Brewery near Queens Wharf, and John Moss behind the Ship Inn in Flinders Lane.[26] Most of these early brewing establishments used local barley and hops, but their product was poor and indigestible.

Melbourne's climate and hot summers made things especially tricky for brewers, who struggled to produce good beer during the summer months when demand was greatest. Efforts to brew in the cooler months also failed because it could not be stored and adequate refrigeration was not possible until the late 1880s. Nevertheless, as Melbourne and its suburbs grew, brewing enterprises expanded and came to dominate Melbourne's inner suburbs, with Collingwood emerging as the brewing precinct.[27]

Before these local breweries popped up around the city, there were only a few breweries in Australia and limited beer options. As such,

Australians succumbed to drinking expensively imported brews. The trend continued well into the new century, with the increasing globalisation of trade evident in the Troedel archive – with brands including Bull Dog Brand from London and Nordhausen Lager Beer, which was imported into Australia from Germany by Schreiber & Schaeffer.

The turning point in beer's epic history came with the arrival of Auguste Joseph François de Bavay (1856-1944), who migrated from Belgium to Melbourne in 1884. De Bavay was a brewer, chemist, bacteriologist and metallurgist and arrived in Melbourne to take up the position of brewer with A & T Aitken of the Victoria Parade Brewery in East Melbourne, which in time became the Victoria Brewery. Thomas Aitken migrated to Australia from Scotland in 1842 and operated the Corio Brewery in Geelong and then Melbourne's Union Brewery before he set up the brewery on Victoria Parade in 1854.

De Bavay was appointed chief brewer in 1884 on a salary of £6 a week with a commission of 1 shilling on every hogshead of good beer, amounting to 238.7 litres.[28] During his tenure, de Bavay established a reputation as an excellent brewer. So much so that he went on to work at Foster's Brewery in 1894, after its director Montague Cohen persuaded de Bavay to join the company as chief brewer.[29] De Bavay's reputation was built upon perfecting the fermentation process. In the 1880s, only the top fermentation process (that is saccharomyces cerevisiae or ale yeast) was available to colonial brewers. De Bavay, well aware of the importance of yeast in the process of brewing beer, began searching for a way of avoiding wild yeasts which caused unwanted secondary and tertiary fermentations.

His first breakthrough came late in 1888 when de Bavay developed 'Melbourne No. 2', which was the first pure yeast used commercially in Australia and possibly the world's first pure culture ever used in top fermentation brewing. He followed this in 1889 with 'Melbourne No.1', which became

<
Elliott's XXX Stout & Ales on Draught (c 1880-1890)
State Library Victoria,
H2000.180/178

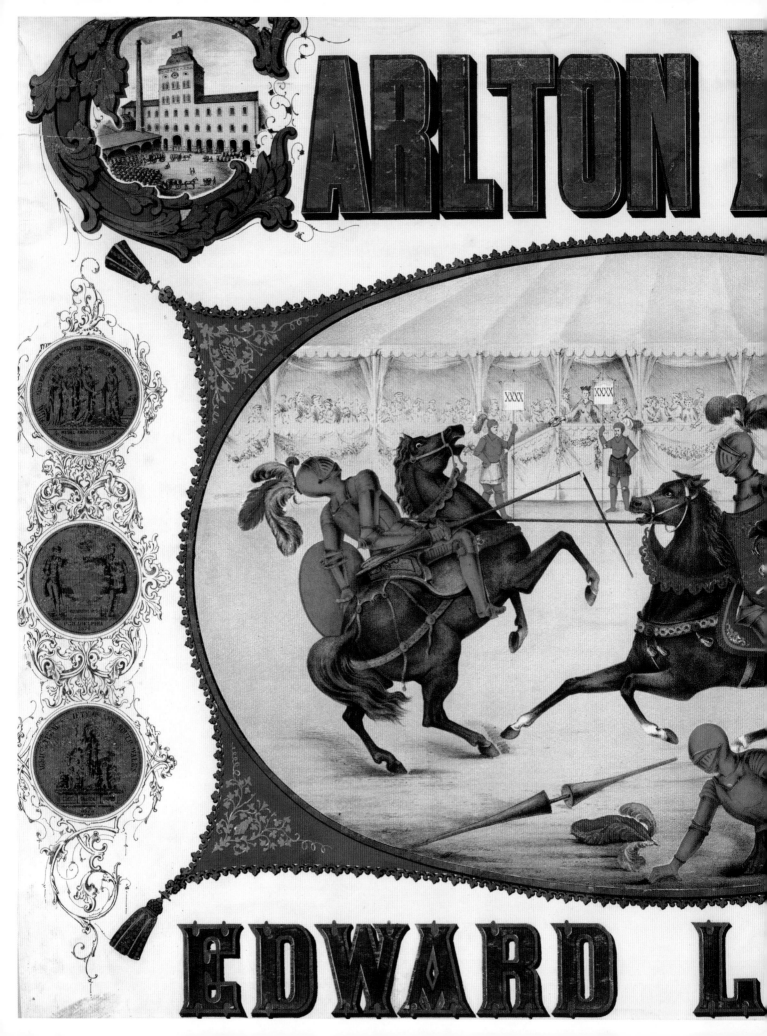

Carlton Prize Ale,
Edward Latham
(c 1875-1883)
State Library Victoria,
H2000.180/255

the basis of Australian brewing. Through his experimentation, de Bavay succeeded in producing a unique Australian beer, establishing Melbourne at the forefront of the existing brewing technology.[30]

In the process of de Bavay's quest for better beer, he discovered the city's water supply was not sanitary. De Bavay believed that Melbourne's fire plugs allowed typhoid bacteria to enter the water supply, producing deadly consequences. He wrote to the editor of *The Argus*, imploring the newspaper to help him in his cause, signing off his letter: 'I am confident that with the help of your valuable paper something may be done to remedy this terrible menace to the public health.'[31]

Through this public campaign and an eventual Royal Commission, de Bavay had new pipes built throughout Melbourne, bringing clean water to the city. He also prevented a typhoid epidemic. Such was his legacy, upon his death in 1944, de Bavay was remembered as doing '... a great deal of scientific work for the purification of Melbourne's water supply.'[32] All of this, for the sake of producing a good brew.

Thanks to stories and successes like de Bavay, foreigners came to try their luck in the local market, as there was a widespread perception that the beer trade was a gateway to wealth, especially since there was no shortage of thirsty customers in Victoria, thanks to the gold rush. Notable among these were Americans W M and R R Foster from New York, who started the Foster Brewing Co in Rokeby Street, Collingwood in 1888, popularising the modern lager style. Edward Latham is another notable name. Latham purchased a small brewery in Bouverie Street, Carlton in 1864 upon his arrival from Liverpool. He sold out in 1883 for a substantial profit, but The Melbourne Brewing & Malting Company lived on.

In *Carlton Brewery: The Melbourne Brewing & Malting Company Limited* (c 1875), the central image shows the new brewery erected in 1873, a red brick building with a tower and flagpole, flying a large red flag with a white A on it. Drawn by Richard Wendel, the courtyard has barrels of beer awaiting collection, and a horse-drawn cart laden with barrels for delivery. Two smaller images fringe the central image, showing other brewing properties. The bluestone Bouverie Street factory on the left, and the bluestone factory in Victoria Street, erected in 1870, on the right. In 1907 it was renamed the Carlton & United Brewery after the amalgamation of the Carlton and Victoria Breweries and the McCracken, Castlemaine, Shamrock and Foster's Breweries.[33]

Carlton & United Brewery (CUB) went on to become Australia's most iconic and enduring brewers. As part of the amalgamation, the firm accumulated all of the brands and trade marks of its competitors. Those involved in the merger understood the value attached to these brands – brands which persist to this day. And more than one hundred years after the merger, CUB still recognises this value, having become entangled in a lengthy legal battle to protect their heritage beer labels.[34]

Richard Wendel
(1851-1926), *Carlton Brewery:
The Melbourne Brewing &
Malting Company Limited*
(c 1875)
State Library Victoria,
H2000.212/3

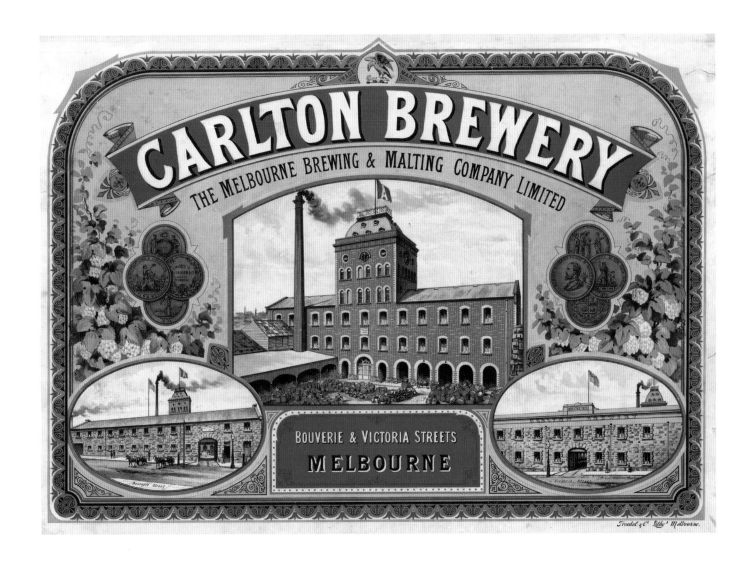

Try the Australian Trent Brewery's Pure Malt & Hop Ales (c 1881-1900)
State Library Victoria, H2000.180/248

Castlemaine Standard Brewing
Coy's Fine Ales
(c 1881-1900)
State Library Victoria,
H2000.180/193

Bull Dog Brand R. Porter & Co.
London (c 1881–1900)
State Library Victoria,
H2000.180/210

Nordhausen Lager Beer. Schreiber & Schaefer. Little Flinders Street, West Melbourne. Sole Agents for Australia (c 1881–1900)
State Library Victoria, H2000.180/203

Teetotalism, Tobacco and the Turn of the Century

The turn of the century was a turbulent time for brewers in Australia, thanks to the depression of the 1890s. Tax increases raised costs for manufacturing, and reduced profits and in response, many breweries were forced to close. There was also an oversupply of Australian brewers, and the competition made the trade less lucrative than it once was. The Society of Melbourne Brewers was formed in 1903 to remedy the failing industry. Their mandate was to set a minimum fixed price for beer. Members of the Society included the breweries that amalgamated and become Carlton & United Breweries in 1907.

The new century also saw rising temperance activity. The temperance movement was a social movement against the consumption of alcoholic beverages. In Australia, the temperance movement began in the mid-1830s, promoting moderation rather than abstinence.[35] This was in direct response to Australia's consumption rates, but also the way that nineteenth century advertising and marketing glamorised alcohol and the drinking culture.

A quick glance at the exquisite pieces in Troedel's collection confirms this – despite growing concerns about the adverse health effects of drinking – with alcoholic beverages described as active and powerful poisons.[36] One doctor went so far as deriding the invention of alcohol in the first place: 'Water was the primitive and original beverage, as it is the only liquid fitted for dilluting (sic), moistening and cooling — the ends of drink appointed by nature; it is sufficient and effectual for all purposes of human wants and drink; and happy: had it been for mankind if other artificial liquors had never been invented.'[37]

Advertising for tobacco and cigarettes took the same form during this period. In fact, there were interesting similarities in the way alcohol and tobacco was advertised, and the temperance movement more generally. From the 1880s to the 1930s, some sectors of society spoke out on the subject of tobacco's deleterious effects on both morals and health, in the same tone and the same strong terms as they did against alcohol. The concern around excessive consumption reached such a frenzy that attempts were made to prohibit alcohol entirely on the Victorian Goldfields in 1852.[38] In recent times, commentators have come to draw parallels with the temperance movement and the anti-tobacco and anti-smoking campaigns of the 1990s.[39] Before this, historians had not given much attention to the links between smoking and drinking, or between temperance and the opposition to smoking.

Anti-tobacco agitation was a natural extension of temperance work, because smoking and drinking often occurred together, particularly in public houses. Smoking and drinking also often accompanied the other in advertising. There were parallels in the way tobacco, and tobacco pipes were advertised. Like alcohol, these advertising posters and labels used bright colours and alluring imagery to draw in the consumer, and are a far cry from the plain packages required by law in Australia today. There was an opulence and grandeur used to frame these ads, to convey the life one could lead if paired with these products. And there was not a health warning in sight. To the contrary, some firms linked tobacco, sport, a healthy lifestyle and success.

The Cricketer (c 1880) perfectly encapsulates Australia's long history of partnering sports and tobacco, before its decoupling in the 1980s. This poster places Australian cricketer Charles Bannerman as the central figure of an advertisement for Cameron Brothers & Co's tobacco. Bannerman was born in 1851 in Kent, England and died in 1930.[40] He represented Australia in three Test matches between 1877 and 1879. He played for New South Wales at a domestic level, and represented Australia in Test cricket before becoming an umpire. Bannerman is most famous for facing the first ball ever bowled in Test cricket, scoring the first run in Test cricket and making the first Test century – with the first Test played between Australia and England at the Melbourne Cricket Ground in March 1877.

SMOKE

CIGARE...
3...
PACK...

*Smoke Smoke Cigarettes
3D Packet* (c 1881–1890)
State Library Victoria,
H2000.180/221

T.C. Williams & Co. Mabel
Cut Plug (c 1881-1890)
State Library Victoria,
H2008.94/48

The Cricketer (c 1880)
State Library Victoria,
Volume 11

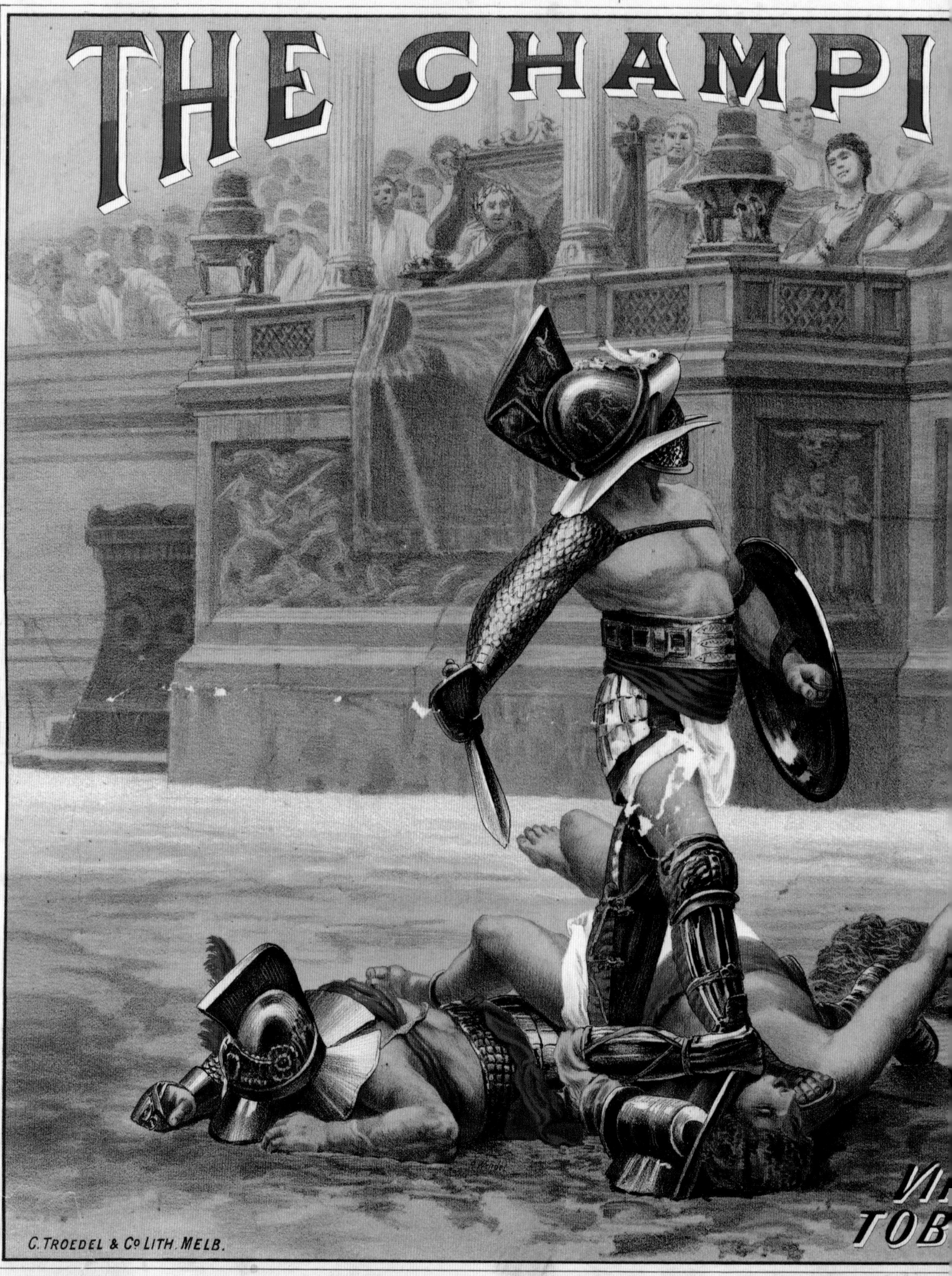
THE CHAMPI
C. TROEDEL & Co LITH. MELB.

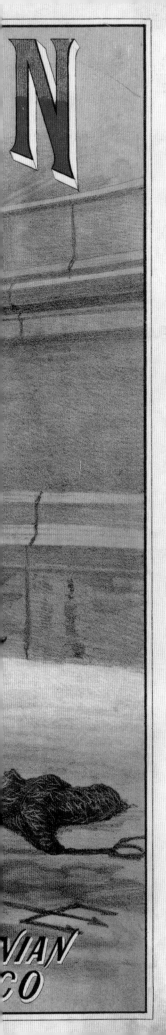

The Champion Virginian Tobacco
(c 1881-1900)
State Library Victoria,
H2000.180/240

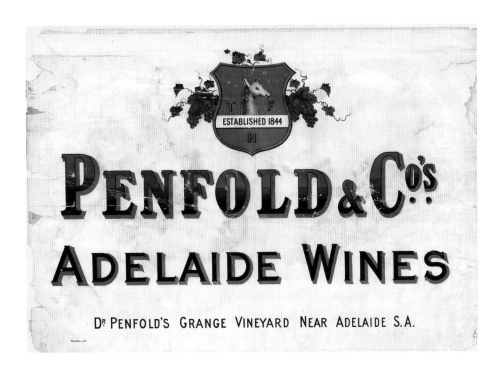

Penfold & Co's Adelaide Wines
(c 1881-1900)
State Library Victoria,
H2000.180/257

In the central image, Bannerman is lining up to face the approaching ball on the Melbourne Cricket Ground. His opposing fieldsman stand in the distance. The Members Stand is positioned behind the players. The border is rimmed with Australian native flora including wattle and eucalyptus trees. Each corner of the poster is bordered by Australian nation icons – cockatoos, possums, emus and kangaroos. A red ribbon spans across the top of the poster, bearing the words 'The Cricketer' – such is the iconic status of Charles Bannerman – there is no need to mention his name.

While ultimately unsuccessful in achieving prohibition in Australia in the long-term, the temperance movement did have some impact in the short-term when it came to developing a market for alcohol alternatives. We can see this in the range of non-alcoholic beverages sold during this period. These products were advertised and glamorised in the same way and in the same style as alcohol but with supposed, added health benefits. Picking up on the threads of the temperance movement is the poster for *Weaver & Co. Dandelion Ale* (c 1881-1890). Weaver & Co's range of hop bitters, aerated waters and cordials were promoted as low-alcohol and non-intoxicating, and were marked as '... the genuine teetotal drink'. Their prize-winning products included ginger wine, orange bitters and quinine champagne, while their hop bitters were portrayed as almost medicinal, with customers encouraged to '[d]rink hop bitters and become the picture of health'.

The alcoholic overtones in *Australian Moet Non-Alcoholic, Prepared by Geo. H. Bennett, Richmond* (c 1881-1890) are clear. One of the most prized items in the Troedel collection, this poster features a clown in a jester's outfit, holding a sign bearing the words 'Australian Non-Alcoholic Moet'. The 42.7 x 28.5 centimetre poster was drawn in the style of the French poster art movement and bears all of the hallmark traits of that style. Perhaps the clown knows that authentic Moët champagne was made in France and was a registered trade mark of Moët & Chandon (who registered dozens of trade marks in Australia during the nineteenth century).[41] This was typical practice for the time, as most traders showed utter disregard for their competitors' branding and trade marks.

These alcohol alternatives were popular for a short period, thanks to the trend of coffee houses.[42] In the 1880s, a number of hotels were built as or converted to coffee palaces, where alcohol was not served – a trend that spread around the world.[43] But with the waning influence of the temperance movement, most of these hotels either applied for liquor licences or were demolished. And Australians turned to drink once again, until war austerity measures were introduced, imposing early closing times as a way to curb consumption.

<
Australian Moet Non-Alcoholic, Prepared by Geo. H. Bennett, Richmond
(c 1881-1890)
State Library Victoria,
H2008.94/88

Penfold's Vineyards
(c 1881-1900)
State Library Victoria,
Volume 19

During this time, Australia began to build the foundations for its world-class wine industry.[44] Australian wines were considered to be '… the most healthful and the most wholesome drink …' and it was even predicted that the prosperity of Australia must sooner or later rest '… on the cultivation of the vine'.[45] Some of Australia's first wines, and most seminal brands are found in the Troedel archive, including Penfolds.

Penfolds was founded in Adelaide in 1844 by Dr Christopher Rawson Penfold, after emigrating to Australia with his wife from Angmering, West Sussex, England. Penfold started out producing fortified wines in the style of sherry and port for his patients. As demand for his wines increased, the winery expanded and was officially established in 1844 at the 500 acre property – Magill Estate.

The Penfolds began their vineyard by planting vine cuttings they carried on their voyage to Australia.[46] The companies Clarets and Rieslings became increasingly popular before Christopher died in 1870, by which stage the vineyard '… had grown to one of the largest in the world'.[47] After his death, Christopher's wife Mary assumed total responsibility for the winery and the business continued to thrive, as it does to this day, with its award winning Grange recognised internationally.

The Troedels had a long association with Penfolds, and continued to print their labels well into the twentieth century. One of the early labels is shown

in *Penfold & Co's Adelaide Wines* (c 1881-1900). In *Penfold's Vineyards* (c 1881-1900), the rolling vineyard at Magill Estate takes centre stage. It was here that Penfolds planted several grape varieties including grenache, verdelho, mataro (mourvedre), frontignac and pedro ximenez.

The South Australian climate proved to be popular for wine. Another local winemaker who achieved success at a rapid rate in the region was Thomas Hardy. Hardy bottled his first vintage in 1857. His tradition and brand has continued for five generations and is still in production today. One of Hardy's early varieties was the internationally recognised OOMOO brand wine.

The label *Hardy's Oomoo and other First Class Adelaide Wines* (c 1881-1900) bears a central oval design with an emu and two kangaroos, with an Aboriginal figure carrying a spear stepping out of the last O in the title. The central design is bordered either side by three medallions won in the colonial and intercolonial exhibitions, between two vertical rows of entwined vines. While the design is styled to exude class and excellence, with the red velvet ribbon draped across the label, the brand was subject to some unsavoury controversy. In fact, the brand name OOMOO was the subject of a legal challenge in the United Kingdom after a competing wine importer and owner of the EMU trade mark objected to its use.

It was alleged that the word OOMOO meant 'choice' in an Australian 'Aboriginal' language and

*Hardy's Oomoo and other
First Class Adelaide Wines*
(c 1881–1900)
State Library Victoria,
H2000.180/194

so, it was not a valid trade mark because it was not distinctive. The matter was heard before Chitty J in 1889. He held that although OOMOO might mean choice to an Aboriginal Australian, it was meaningless to the ordinary Englishman in that country.[48] As such, Chitty found that OOMOO was a fancy word not in common use under the terms of the *Patents, Designs and Trade Marks Act 1883* (UK), and so, it could be registered as a label for wine by the British wine importer Peter Burgoyne.

In making his finding, Chitty J ignored a study which pointed to the Indigenous meaning of the word, and instead found that the word was manufactured and meaningless to an ordinary Englishman, or a sufficient number of Englishman, as evidenced by the fact that '… nobody that I know has ever asked for "a glass of Oomoo".[49]

The consequences of this Victorian decision still reverberate across today's cosmopolitan world, and its reasoning continues to guide the law relating to foreign language trade marks.[50] The case also highlights the broader historical trend of cultural appropriation in advertising, and how the courts and the legal system validated this behaviour. The decision also encapsulates the ongoing oppression of Indigenous Australians. The presumed lack of knowledge of barbarous language[51] meant that British traders could pursue their practice of appropriating indigenous symbols, taking scenes of the empire into every corner of the British home,[52] with the imprimatur of the trade mark registration system, and ultimately the law.[53]

Weaver & Co. Dandelion Ale (c 1881–1890)
State Library Victoria,
H2008.94/38

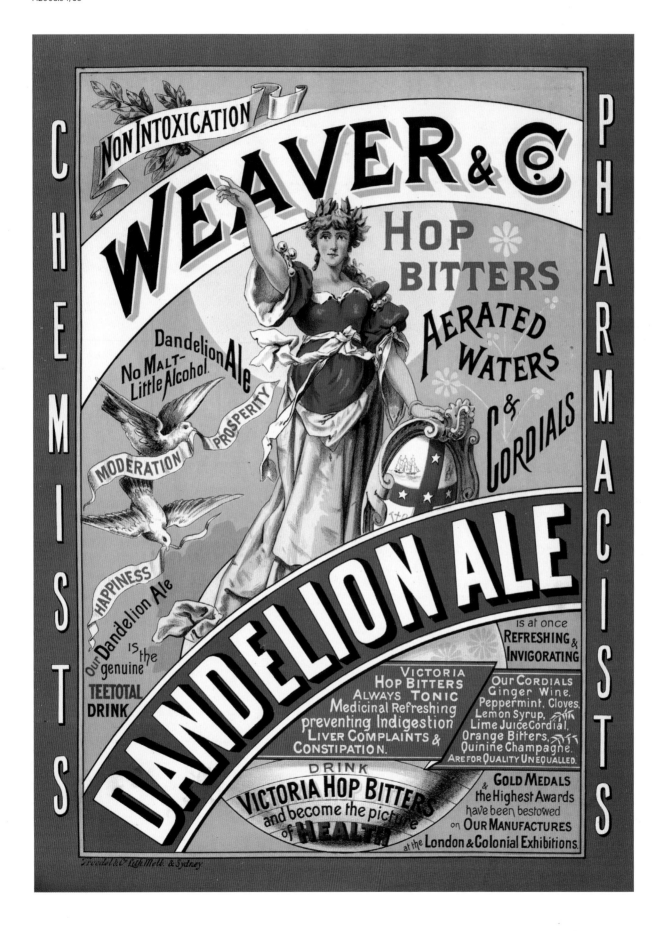

Japanese Yum Yum or
Compound Fruit Extract (c 1881-1890)
State Library Victoria,
H2008.94/36

IV
Health and Hygiene

^
Pearl Cream (1875)
State Library Victoria,
H96.160/2255

The nineteenth century saw a growing demand for personal products used in the pursuit of health and wellbeing. The result was a flourishing market for medical preparations, pharmaceuticals and related hygiene products including common soap and laundry soap – and ipso facto – a rich collection of labels, posters and beautifully crafted trade cards for these products. The juxtaposition of style and subject matter was stunning, with these artefacts combining fine design with disinfectant and disease. The Troedel archive provides some captivating examples.

The poster *Little's "Phenyle" Disinfectants Best and Safest* (c 1870-1879) shows a farmer leaning on a fence and smoking a pipe. There is a sheepdog in the foreground, with rolling pastures and a farmhouse perched on the hill into the distance. The product name is printed across the palings in bright yellow paint. The scenic illustration used for this poster, which could have equally been framed and hung on a wall in a living room gallery such was its elegance, formed part of a series produced by Troedel & Co.

Little's "Phenyle" Disinfectants (c 1870-1879) is another poster from the series, produced during the same period. It is also set in the country and features the same farmer. This time, the man is sitting atop a horse, with his sheepdog trailing behind. He passes by a bushman with his swag who is sitting by the side of the road, taking a rest stop and smoking a pipe. The bushman is also accompanied by his sheepdog, who sits loyally beside him. The two men share an exchange before the farmer goes on his way, facing a choice at the crossroad ahead, marked 'HEALTH' and 'SAFETY'. The fences which line either side of the path are inscribed with the product's details.

Both of these posters show the atmospheric tone and texture typical of the lithograph. The illustrator is unknown, but both were likely produced in the late 1870s or early 1880s given Little's Phenyle Disinfectant was widely promoted in the press at around that time '[f]or flushing all kinds of sewers … and general use in all cases of sickness …'[1] It was also advertised for use to prevent typhoid and other diseases.[2] The product was commonly used in kitchens and toilets but it was also used to sanitise dairy milk handling rooms, which explains the country setting used in these posters.

Little's disinfectants were historically significant to the Kiewa Valley, a mostly rural community near the alpine regions of Victoria rural with out-houses and milk collection areas that required routine sanitation.[3] It is no coincidence then that the views depicted in Troedel's posters for the brand bear a striking resemblance to the Kiewa Valley landscape. The products were also sold throughout cities in Australia, through local agents appointed by Morris Little & Son, the chemical company responsible for producing the disinfectant in Doncaster, England and who exported it around the world.

The company registered numerous trade marks in Australia, such was the extent of their trade, including LITTLE'S PHENYLE SOLUBLE DISINFECTANT, LITTLE'S SANITARY PHENYLE POWDER, and LITTLE'S PATENT FLUID DIP NON-POISONOUS.[4] Other marks include LITTLE'S PHENYLE DOG SOAP and LITTLE'S PHENYLE SOAP.[5] The company's embrace of branding is alluded to in the poster *Little's "Phenyle" Disinfectants Best and Safest*, with the words 'TRADE MARK' inscribed on the trunk of the tree against which the bushman is resting, above and below a sign marked 'C. H. 6. S.' a kookaburra sits perched on the branch above.

Phenyle is a phonetic play on the word phenol, a chemical compound primarily used as a disinfectant. Also known as carbolic acid, Phenyle was used as a product name by Morris Little & Son and other chemical companies – a marketing technique that started to gain traction in the late nineteenth century, leading to the proliferation of unique brand names. Carbolic acid is still used as a disinfectant today, although with more caution, with reports of poisoning by carbolic acid a regular news item in the nineteenth century.[6]

The beauty of the Australian countryside depicted in these advertising posters masked this ugly reality. The posters also hint at the hyperbolic marketing practices used to promote these types of poisonous products. The samples contained in the Troedel archive expose this trend, with the sale of magic cure-all remedies boasting superlatively claims emblematic of the pharmaceutical marketplace. So while today, the chemical and drug industry is highly regulated, lawmakers in the nineteenth century were only just being confronted with this regulatory dilemma. Marketers and advertisers, therefore, had free-reign to exploit the credulity of the sick and vulnerable through puffery and the sale of patent medicines, which were not the subject of patent protection at all.

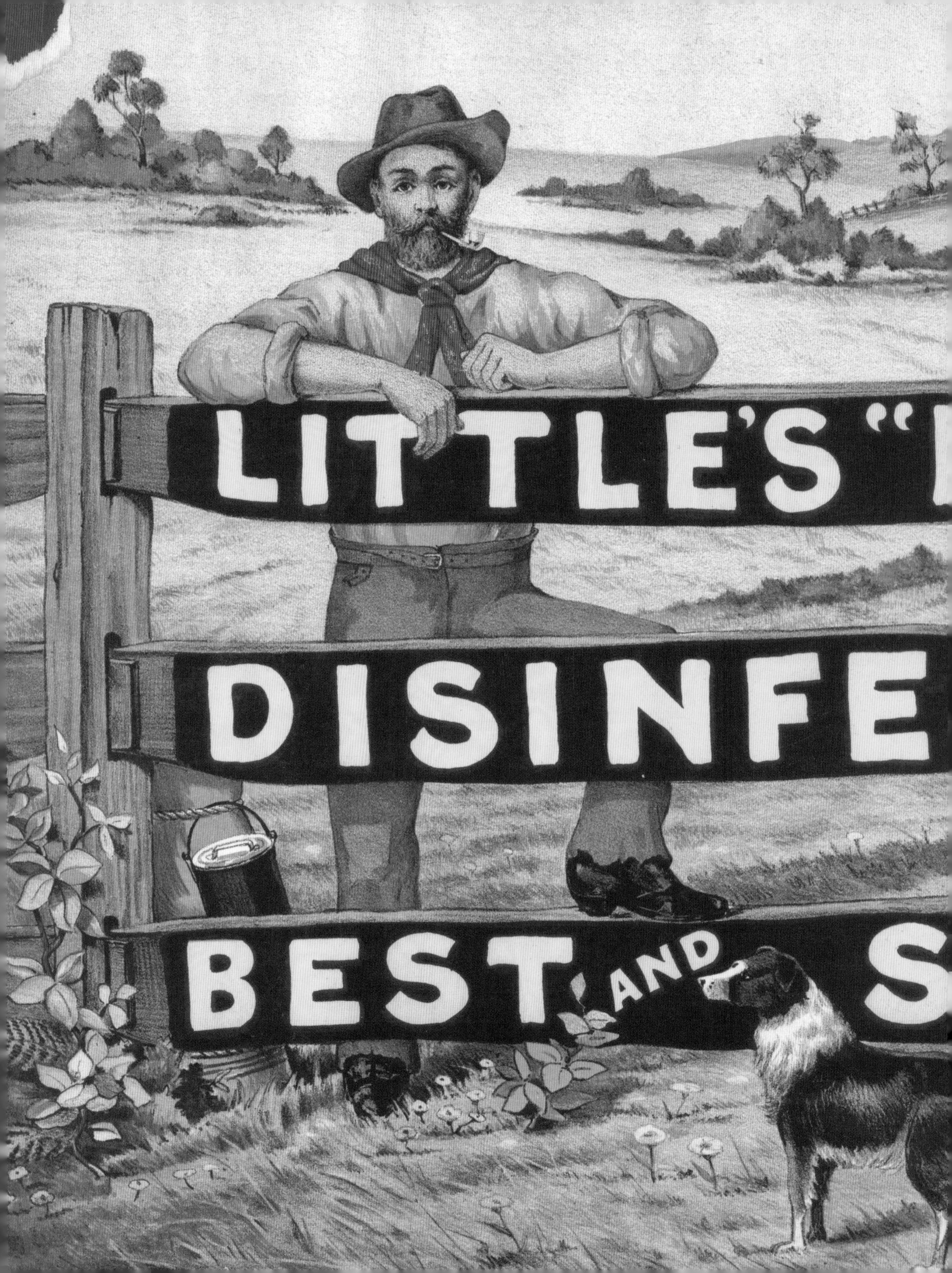
LITTLE'S "
DISINFE
BEST AND S

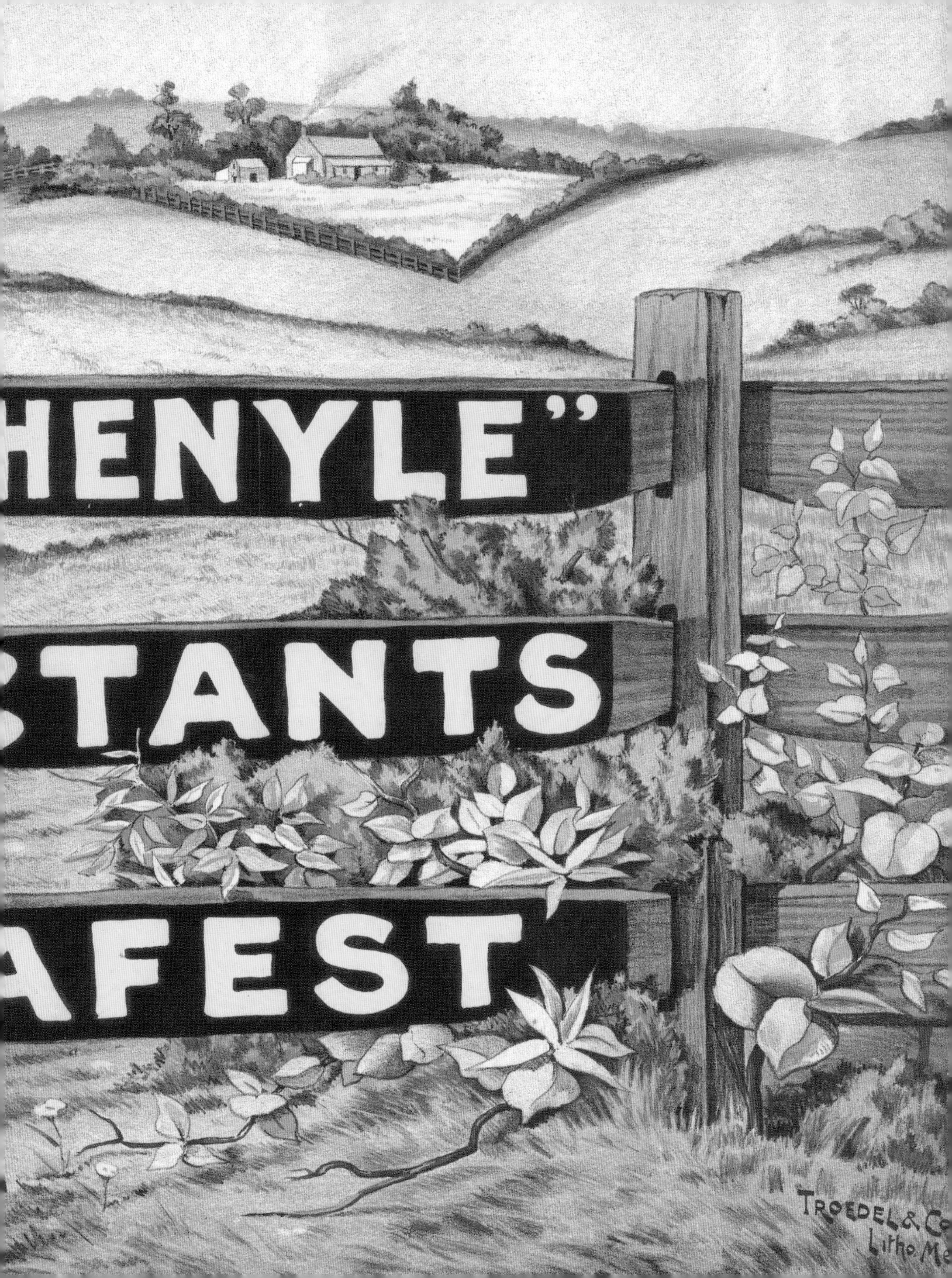
HENYLE"
STANTS
AFEST
TROEDEL & Co
Litho Me

^
Little's "Phenyle"
Disinfectants Best and Safest
(c 1870-1879)
State Library Victoria,
H2000.180/113

Puffery and Patent Medicines

Troedel's archive provides a window into the unregulated territory of patent medicines and untruths in pharmaceutical advertising. These products were advertised as unproven cures and antidotes for every ailment known to humankind and were frequently endorsed by individuals purporting to be doctors but who had no medical qualifications at all. They were also promoted using claims and statements based in pseudo-science, and pure puffery.

Puffery is a well-known trick of the advertising trade and has its roots in the nineteenth century. Puffery usually consists of '... an exuberant endorsement of a lacklustre product.'[7] As puffery claims are subjective, they often appear as an advertisement in disguise, sometimes masquerading as a news story or an opinion piece.[8] Doctors or chemists occasionally put their face and name on products to promote themselves as manufacturers with repute, good standing and a concern for their patients. In reality, these people usually had no medical training, and they most certainly had no involvement in the manufacture of these treatments, nor could they vouch for their effectiveness.

Ralph Potts Well Known Magic Balm (c 1880) is a classic example of pharmaceutical puffery. This 29.1 x 47.0 centimetre poster was produced circa 1880 and did not attempt to exalt the medical or scientific qualities of the product being advertised. Instead, the mystical healing properties of this balm took centre stage, next to a portrait of Ralph Potts. Potts imported *Magic Balm* into the Australian colonies from New York, and sold his elixir through local agents and shopkeepers. He also administered the balm on patients in his dental practice.

Potts' foray into dentistry was unconventional. He established a dental practice in Perth and even assigned himself the title of Dental King – all this from a man with no dental qualifications.[9] His professional track record was recounted in his obituary, along with the controversy he courted along the way: 'Mr Potts adopted an unusual method of introducing himself as a dentist. From a flare-lighted platform on a block where now stands the offices of the Electricity and Gas Department in Murray Street he employed girls to run along the planks and sell his "magic balm", the virtues of which he extolled. Then he invited anyone suffering from toothache to step up and have the offending molar painlessly removed for one shilling. After difficulty he got registration and from then conducted surgeries in various parts of the city.'[10]

The difficulty referred to in Potts' obituary were charges laid against him by the Dental Board for breaches of the *Dentists Act 1894* (WA).[11] The Dental Board took objection to the way Potts advertised his services and his use of the Dental King moniker because it would '... tend to make people believe he was a duly qualified man'.[12] The Board was also concerned about Potts performing dental procedures without qualification.

Potts travelled around the colonies trading under the Dental King title, and was reportedly accompanied by a brass band.[13] Potts started selling magic balm and other pills, while extracting teeth on the streets and in public places in and around Sydney and South Australia in the 1880s. When he arrived in Perth, he applied for registration as a dental practitioner but was refused as the Dental Board was not satisfied that Potts had acquired any qualifications in Australia or elsewhere in the world, finding that the qualification Potts held in New South Wales was obtained from an 'unrecognised association'.[14]

A few years later and Potts came before the courts again for additional breaches of the Dentists Act 1894 (WA). This time, he was charged for extracting a woman's teeth without qualification. Potts was fined £10 and £5 16s 6d costs.[15] Nevertheless, Potts continued his dealings as a dentist, advertising himself as the secretary

<
Little's "Phenyle" Disinfectants (c 1870-1879)
State Library Victoria,
H2000.180/154

Richard Wendel (1851-1926),
*Ralph Potts Well Known Magic
Balm* (c 1880)
State Library Victoria,
H2000.180/153

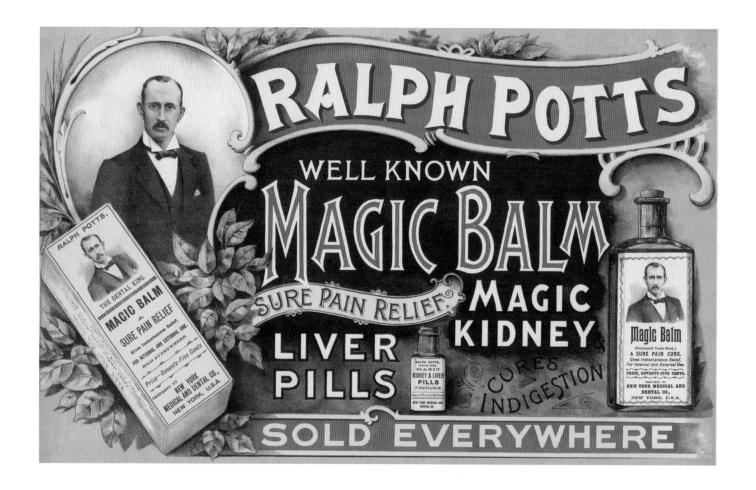

to the New York Dental Institute, and running a dentistry business under this name in Perth.[16] His persistence and utter disregard for authority paid off. In time, the Colonial Secretary ordered the Board to register Potts as a dentist,[17] and he went on to have a distinguished career in dentistry. He was also an active participant in several local community organisations and was a Member of Perth City Council for some time.

Potts' colourful past was hidden from the public, who were instead dazzled by this colourful poster and the exquisite craftsmanship of Richard Wendel, who was responsible for the artwork. While it is easy to judge Potts and his questionable marketing tactics today, they were common for that time. These types of advertisements for magic bullet medicines appeared before any regulation of the industry, and so firms were able to manufacture and sell all manner of medicines and devices without any regard to their effectiveness. And early attempts to regulate these kinds of practices in the *Dentists Act 1894* (WA) and its colonial equivalents were futile.[18] The protracted litigation brought by the Dental Board against Potts is proof of this.

The lack of regulation, or at least effective regulation, meant that these kinds of advertisements were not the exception but the rule. It also meant firms were able to use all manner of ingredients, including opium, alcohol, morphine and cocaine, mercury and turpentine, leading to intoxication, addiction and sometimes death.[19] One well-known example was *Dr Collis Browne's Chlorodyne*, which reportedly contained six grains of morphine and six grains of cannabis extract, all of which were not disclosed on the label.[20] Another example is *Clarke's Blood Mixture*, which was sold in the Australian colonies with the tag line – 'for the blood is life' – a quote from *The Book of Deuteronomy*, which is mentioned and ridiculed in the book *Dracula*.

Clarke's Blood Mixture was advertised to treat a range of ailments including sores, glandular swelling, skin complaints, scrofula, scurvy, cancerous ulcers, bad legs, rheumatism, gout, sore eyes, dropsy, pimples, blackheads and piles. Developed by chemist Francis Jonathan Clarke in the 1860s in Lincoln, England, the mixture was spruiked as a 'World Famed Blood Mixture'[21] and 'the Greatest Medicine ever discovered'.[22] Generally, these ads were accompanied by outrageous testimonials from patients claiming to

be completely healed of their illness.[23]

It later transpired that *Clarke's Blood Mixture* exploited consumers' vulnerability with its wild curative claims but also in its pricing. In 1909, the British Medical Association estimated the cost of its ingredients was the equivalent of half a penny compared to the sales cost, which was 14 pence in modern terms.[24] The British Medical Association also found the product contained traces of chloroform and ammonia, putting customers' health at risk.

This was consistent with condemnations made in 1895, when the editors of *Exposures to Quackery* warned of the severe health implications posed by the product. Following an examination of an eight-ounce bottle of *Clarke's Blood Mixture* conducted in 1875, the product was found to contain iodide of potash, chloric ether, potash, and water which had been coloured with burnt sugar. According to this study, at the recommended dosage, patients would develop iodism – a condition causing inflammation of the mucous membranes of the eyes and nose, salivation, purging and nausea.[25]

At the other end of the spectrum were remedies containing herbs, fruit extracts and all natural ingredients. These products were also ineffective. In fact, they had no healing properties at all. Some examples include Moulton's Fruit Pills or Weston's Magic Pills.[26] Another example was Eno's Fruit Salts. This product was the subject of a trade mark dispute, where a chemist gave evidence that he was '… sorry to say that there was any fruit in the preparation. If there were anything in it [sic] it was tartaric acid …' which was probably derived from wine.[27]

Some companies deliberately tried to set themselves apart from these unscrupulous practices by promoting their products as safe alternatives to those offered by their competitors. In a series of advertisements produced by Troedel for *Moulton's Blood Searcher, The Great Blood Purifier* (1851-1885), a disclaimer against the use of toxic substances was displayed prominently, with the proprietor emphasising the purity of their products which contained '… no Mercury, Minerals, or Deleterious Drugs, and Warranted to effect a Positive Cure'. The disclaimer was nevertheless still coupled with outrageously broad and unsubstantiated assertions about how the product '[s]trikes at the root of the disease by purifying the

Moulton's Blood Searcher,
The Great Blood Purifier
(c 1851–1885)
State Library Victoria,
H32088/55

MOULTON'S BLOOD SEARCHER,
THE GREAT BLOOD PURIFIER.

Health and Beauty; Strong and Pure Rich Blood;
Increase of Flesh and Weight: Clear Skin and Beautiful
Complexion secured to all.

The great cure for all Chronic, Scrofulous, Constitut-
ional, and Skin Diseases. Purely vegetable, containing
no Mercury, Minerals, or Deleterious Drugs, and Warranted to effect a Positive Cure.

Price 2s, 6d.

C. E. MOULTON, Sole Proprietor,
MELBOURNE and SYDNEY.

Moulton's Blood Searcher,
The Great Blood Purifier
(c 1851-1885)
State Library Victoria,
H32088/54

blood, restoring the liver and kidneys to healthy action, and invigorating the nervous system'.[28]

These prints were part of the album of *Australian Tradesmen's Tickets*, which was compiled by Edward Gilks. Gilks was a sketcher, lithographer and draughtsman who migrated to Australia from London in 1853. He is best known for his many engravings, watercolours and lithographs of Melbourne's most significant buildings and events. Gilks spent a period working as the government lithographer, but he also collaborated with Troedel on 'The Melbourne Album', producing the prints *Elizabeth Street* (1864) and *Flinders Street* (1864).[29] He continued his association with Troedel and produced some commercial works too, such as these simple but meticulously drawn sketches for *Moulton's Blood Searcher* (c 1851-1885).

Moulton's was a household name in the Australian colonies, with the Charles Moulton name adorning a variety of medical preparations. As well as Moulton's Fruit Pills and Moulton's renowned Blood Searcher, the company also sold the popular Pain Paint which purported to heal a variety of ailments '[n]o matter how violent or excruciating the pain, the Rheumatic, Bedridden, Infirm, Crippled, Nervous, Neuralgic, or prostrated with disease, may suffer.'[30]

Pain Paint was sold with the promise of curing all pain and affording instant ease and relief, with labels for the product found in Troedel's catalogue. This message also appeared in the many newspaper advertisements for Pain Paint, including a classified placed in *The Bulletin* which featured the headline 'Cures All Pain'.[31] Ironically, on the very next page was a satirical poem titled 'Quacks and Their Victims'.[32] The first verse unapologetically mocks the likes of Moulton and his advertisement for Pain Paint and the myriad of similar ads that filled the pages of the publication, which would '... [h]int at disease, and then announce a cure.'[33]

Moulton's Pain Paint was also advertised as 'Registered and Patented'.[34] The newspapers even referred to its inventor as '... the proprietor of a patent medicine ...'[35] While it is true that Moulton did apply to register the words PAIN PAINT as a special and distinctive trade mark in Victoria,[36] there is no evidence of any patent application ever recorded in the Victorian Government Gazette.

Puffery went hand in hand with patent medicine claims. Patent medicines, sometimes referred to as nostrums, quack and alternative medicines, were sold over the counter without a prescription. These medicines were popular in the late nineteenth and early twentieth century and were designed for self-medication, providing a convenient remedy for the general population who did not have access to competent medical care, doctors or well-trained chirurgeons. They were also an attractive alternative for those suspicious of the medical profession. While there was a time when these products were sold as legitimate treatments for a variety of ailments '... it was not long before the spirit of creative salesmanship seized the imaginations of the patent-medicine advertisement writer ...' who embraced '... a host of wild claims for promoting the use of the nostrum of the hour.'[37]

The patent medicine description was problematic for several reasons. Most of these products were not patented at all. This practice dates back to *Sykes v Sykes*, one of the earliest reported common law trade mark cases.[38] In this 1824 case, Sykes brought an action against another trader who marked their shot-belts and powder-flasks with the words SYKES PATENT in imitation of his use of the same words on his shot-belts and powder flasks. The Court upheld a verdict for Sykes concluding that the competing trader had violated his rights by marking their goods as if they were manufactured by Sykes and selling them to retailers for the express purpose of being resold as the goods of Sykes. This was even though the plaintiff's product was not patented.

Genuine patent medicines originated in England as proprietary medicines manufactured under grants or patents of royal favours to those who provided medicine to Royalty – these grants being the precursor to the modern patent system. The history of patent medicines trace back to the seventeenth century in England and the Crown's issue of a patent for Anderson's Scots Pills.[39] These medicines were exported to the world including America and the British colonies, but colonists quickly discovered it was cheaper to make these products locally, and so a local industry was born.

Patent medicines were often advertised with a list of undisclosed ingredients. Of course, this makes no sense, because if these products were patented, then the patent process would have required disclosure of this information, which would have been made available to the public on the patent registers which were in force in the Australian colonies by the 1850s.[40] In any event, manufacturers were not legally obligated to label the contents of their medicines, which explains why the use of toxic and addictive ingredients was rife.

The patent tag was also used to emphasise a royal connection to exaggerate the remedial qualities of the products being advertised. From the earliest times in England, there was no government agency charged with verifying that these products were useful or sage. Moreover, there was no statute limiting the sorts of claims that could be made in advertising.[41] As a result, the nineteenth century medicine cabinet was filled with lies, and so were the newspapers. Columns of print space were devoted to advertisements for patent medicines claiming to cure almost every ailment in existence, and those that were not yet known to the medical profession.

For these reasons, patent medicines enjoyed an unchecked existence. Attempts were made to regulate these unscrupulous practices. The *Pharmacy Act 1876* (Vic) and the *Poisons Act 1862* (Vic) made significant inroads in Victoria, with both Acts introduced to protect the public from the sale of dangerous toxic goods and addictive substances. The *Pharmacy Act 1876* (Vic) established the Pharmacy Board of Victoria. It also made provision for the registration of pharmaceutical chemists, who were qualified to carry on the business of a chemist and druggist or homeopathic chemist for the compounding and dispensing of prescriptions.

Despite best intentions, and as with the introduction of legislation to regulate dental practices, initial attempts to regulate the pharmaceutical industry were mostly ineffective. Indeed, these practices endured, even after Federation. In 1907, a Royal Commission on Secret Drugs, Cures and Foods condemned the patent medicine industry, observing that '[t]he practices above named … are not partly right, they are entirely wrong, and rooted and grounded in greed.'[42] The Troedel print collection provides a small snapshot of these practices and the objects in question.

Sunlight Soap. Largest Sale in the World. Used in Her Majesty's Laundry (c 1881-1890)
State Library Victoria,
H2000.180/120

Innovation in Bathing and Laundry

As well as a growing medicinal and pharmaceutical market, the nineteenth century saw a new market for soap emerge in the Australian colonies, for both personal use and in the laundry. These products were no longer considered a luxury, but a necessity. As a result, the soap industry became a marketing battlefield, leading to the development of innovative branding and trade-marking practices, and eventually the brand name – including the most iconic brand name in soap – SUNLIGHT SOAP.[43]

Sunlight Soap was the premier brand of Lever Brothers. The company was founded in Britain in 1885 by William Hesketh Lever and was built on an idea developed with his brother James Darcy Lever, for the production of a free lathering laundry soap made of glycerine and vegetable oils rather than the commonly used tallow. The idea revolutionised hygiene practices in Victorian England, making cleanliness commonplace. Lever Brothers built an empire on its innovative methods for soap production but also gained notoriety for its unique branding strategy. Lever Brothers was one of the first to adopt the brand name as a trade mark. This set Lever Brothers apart from its competitors and contributed to its success as the world leader in the highly competitive common soap market.

Like so many other enterprises of its time and its closest competitors, Lever Brothers was a family business, growing from small beginnings to become the most dominant soap manufacturer in the United Kingdom and abroad. The brothers bought a small soap works in 1885 in Warrington, England, where they began producing what was to become its signature Sunlight Soap. By 1888, the factory in Warrington was producing Sunlight Soap at a rate of 450 tons per week.[44] In order to accommodate the burgeoning business, larger premises were built on marshes at Bromborough Pool on the Wirral Peninsula, which later became known as Port Sunlight.[45] Lever Brothers continued to expand, with subsidiaries set up around the world, including in the United States, Switzerland, Canada and Germany. Subsidiaries were also established in Balmain in New South Wales in 1895 and New Zealand in 1919.

While the firm's competitors had produced tablets of toilet soap using device style marks or stamped with fanciful names such as HONEY, PRIMROSE, MUSK and ALMOND suffixed to their company name, Lever Brothers took a novel approach – adopting the distinctive brand – SUNLIGHT.[46] Sunlight was different from the traditional names used by others in the industry, which were not proprietary and usually made reference to colour, scent, or quality. The firm registered the Sunlight brand name as a trade mark in Britain and around the world.[47] These registrations have been maintained to this day, as the Sunlight brand lives on, coupled with its distinctive blue packaging. That striking blue colour was used in *Sunlight Soap. Largest Sale in the World. Used in Her Majesty's Laundry* (c 1881-1890), a poster produced by Troedel & Co sometime in the 1880s, as part of the company's Australian advertising campaign.

Over time, Lever Brothers expanded its catalogue of registered marks using the same strategy, with brands including LIFEBUOY disinfecting soap (1894), LUX soap flakes (1899) and MONKEY scouring powder (1899). And so the brand name was born. Before the brand name, soap manufacturers relied upon beautifully drawn and delicately decorated lithographs to dazzle consumers, based on oil paintings and original works produced by the art departments of printing houses. These firms also relied on racial stereotypes and the commodification of traditional cultures in order to advance the Empire and export colonialism around the world.

The marketing campaign for soap products was greatly assisted by the rapid urbanisation of the major cities and changing living and working conditions. Industrialisation raised new concerns around dirt and disorder. It also brought with it a greater understanding of the benefits of hygiene. But cleanliness was more than a question of hygiene. It became a signpost for moral and social standing – '[c]leanliness, like good manners became an indicator of respectability while dirt and squalor were seen as threats to moral as well as physical health.'[48] The prevailing attitude in Victorian times saw cleanliness equated with respectability and civility and smell and odour an indicator of health, class and social status.

The push for good health, hygiene, personal grooming and self-care was not entirely a natural consequence of industrialisation and urbanisation. Some say the phenomenon was the conscious creation of those who stood to profit from the message – the manufacturers of such health and hygiene products.[49] Before the advertising age and the campaign to educate the public on the need to pay greater attention to their hygiene, bathing was considered a form of debauchery or as an opportunity for the devil to enter your body. Despite attempts to convince the public otherwise, many still believed that bathing was unnecessary and even unhealthy, as it enabled disease.

The public eventually bought into this rhetoric, and by the second half of the nineteenth century, the soap and toiletries industry was well established in the United Kingdom, first for laundry or toilet soap and later for common soap for bathing. The industry was fiercely competitive, with many firms establishing themselves first in the United Kingdom before building a presence overseas, including in the Australian colonies. With this fierce competition came accusations of underselling and tactics of unfair competition.[50] This included giving excessive discounts, rebates or credits to customers, providing extra allowances to customers on large orders, booking forward customer orders and taking orders at old prices. Some manufacturers even provided customers with cash gifts, supplied soap products overweight or supplied the same soap under a different name at a reduced price.[51]

Given the competitiveness of the industry and the vast number of competitors vying for the dominant market position, there was an obvious inclination for manufacturers to differentiate their products and brands to obtain a competitive edge. Indeed, the soap industry was one of the most innovative when it came to product innovation, branding and marketing. Part of this process involved the registration of trade marks. Soap manufacturers flooded the British trade mark register in the late nineteenth century, with names like Lever Brothers, A & F Pears, Joseph Crosfield

and Sons Ltd, and William Gossage leading the way for their laundry soap and common soap products.[52]

Most of the early registered marks were graphical, consistent with the general trend in trade marking practices for that time. That was before the styling evolved to more word-based marks and then brand names, such as SUNLIGHT, as the definition of a trade mark shifted from purely visual marks to fancy or invented words.[53] These trade marks were then used in elaborate global advertising campaigns, which were unique to the soap industry and combined art and advertising to great effect.

A & F Pears was one of the first soap companies to popularise the use of original paintings in advertising, a technique that filtered down to others in the industry. The turning point came in 1886, when the Chairman of A & F Pears, Thomas Barratt reportedly paid £2,200 for an oil painting of a young boy by John Everett Millais and titled *A Child's World*. The original work, which was modelled by the artists' five-year-old grandson William Milbourne James, was exhibited in 1886 at the Grosvenor Gallery in London. It shows a young boy with golden hair looking up at a bubble, holding a bowl of soapy water in his lap. At the foot of the boy, is a terracotta pot, fallen and broken into pieces on the floor. Drawing on vanitas imagery and the still life paintings of sixteenth and seventeenth centuries in Flanders and the Netherlands, Millais' work symbolises the beauty and fragility of life.

After obtaining Millais' permission, although the nature of the permission is disputed, the work was reproduced as a lithograph by the company. The original work was faithfully replicated, with some small but significant additions. The first addition is a young thriving pot plant, on one side of the boy, to counterbalance the broken pot that sits on the other side. The second and most significant addition is a bar of Pears Soap which appears in the foreground, with the brand name embossed on the product in full view of the observer.

The work was printed more than a million times by A & F Pears under the title *Bubbles*.[54] The image was later accompanied by the slogan 'Good morning. Have you used Pears' soap?' The catchphrase was the work of Barratt, and became a well-known colloquialism in the twentieth century. For his success, Barratt became known as the father of modern advertising. After the

Lewis & Whitty's Sun Soap
(c 1881-1890)
State Library Victoria,
H2008.94/77

success of the *Bubbles* advertising campaign, illustrators came to dominate the advertising scene, not only in Britain but also overseas, as many of these businesses sought to build a presence in the colonies, including Australia, bringing their successful advertising campaigns with them.

By the latter part of the nineteenth century, the Australian public came to be educated about the importance of hygiene and cleanliness, contributing to the thriving local soap industry. The Australian Health Society, established in Melbourne by Unitarian Minister Martha Turner in 1875, published brochures and conducted public meetings to educate the poor on issues of health and hygiene, as part of a broader campaign to explain the virtues of bathing and the importance of soap.[55] A number of other publications emerged as authoritative sources relating to health matters including the *Manual of Health & Temperance*, which was published in 1891 by the Health Department and used as an aid for health checks in Victorian schools.[56]

A few years later, in *The Art of Living in Australia*, a handbook for everyday life, Philip E Muskett wrote about the benefits of regular bathing at length: 'The cold bath, at any rate during the summer months, should always be there before breakfast, but in the cooler part of the year the shock may be lessened, if it be desirable, by using tepid water instead of cold. And since there is, as we have seen, a good deal of oily matter excreted by the skin, it becomes necessary to use something in addition to water for cleansing purposes, for the latter is unable to displace the greasy collection by itself. The only thing which will render it easy of removal is soap, as by its action it softens the oily material and dislodges it from the skin. Soap has acquired an evil reputation which it certainly does not deserve, and if it disagrees it is either due to the fact of its being an inferior article, or else the skin itself must be at fault. The best soap to use is the white, not the mottled, Castile, as it is made from pure olive oil. By the proper and judicious use of soap the skin is kept soft and natural, and the complexion is maintained in the hue of health.'[57]

In conveying this message to the Australian public, advertisers combined art with advertising, as the British had before them. Troedel & Co, who was renowned for employing talented artists in the art department, was well placed to accommodate their clients and as such, produced an expansive and elaborate collection of advertising posters for soap products. These ads mostly featured women, who in their role as wives and paid keepers of the household, were considered the appropriate target market, especially for laundry soaps and starch. The depiction of women in these advertisements usually drew on one of either two stereotypes – the hardened help or the ethereal. They also featured bold and bright colours, with Troedel & Co taking full advantage of the crisp colour possibilities that lithography and chromolithography offered.

The image of the woman as the hired help was used in *Lewis & Whitty's Diamond Starch* (1881-1890) which depicted a strong bodied woman with a friendly face. The poster was 53.7 x 37.8 centimetre in size and shows a housemaid in a blue dress, white cap and apron with a red trim, holding up a packet of Diamond Starch in her right hand, and a white waist petticoat with a lace trim flounce in her left hand. A companion poster titled *Lewis & Whitty's Square Blue* (1881-1890) was 55.8 x 35.7 centimetre in size and printed on cream paper. In this poster the housemaid is wearing a bright red velvet skirt and blouse, which is partially covered by a navy blue vest. She is also wearing a devious smile, pointing to a freshly washed bedsheet hanging on the washing line. So well laundered is the bedsheet, one can see the silhouette of a man stealing a kiss from a young women – a secret that is only revealed by using Lewis & Whitty's Square Blue washing powder.

Some of these posters were on display at the company's exhibit at the Sydney showgrounds for the Royal Sydney Show. *The Australian Town and Country Journal* described it as '... one of the prettiest, if not the prettiest of the numerous and varied exhibits in the pavilion, and ... this was the opinion of the judges ... by their awarding it a special certificate for general excellence of exhibit – an honor [sic] which was fully merited.'[58]

Lewis & Whitty's rice starch was regarded as the best in the colony. The company's market dominance was given monopoly status by the press because '... no one but Messrs Lewis and Whitty have succeeded in making it of a quality that commends it to the household.'[59] John B Whitty was born in Dublin, and in 1850 came to Melbourne with his parents. After a short stint working in a stock and station agent's office, he had a chance meeting with Fred Lewis (who would later be a pallbearer at Troedel's funeral), and joined him in his manufacturing business.[60] From humble beginnings in North Melbourne, they built up a

<
Lewis & Whitty's Diamond Starch (c 1881-1890)
State Library Victoria,
H2000.212/12

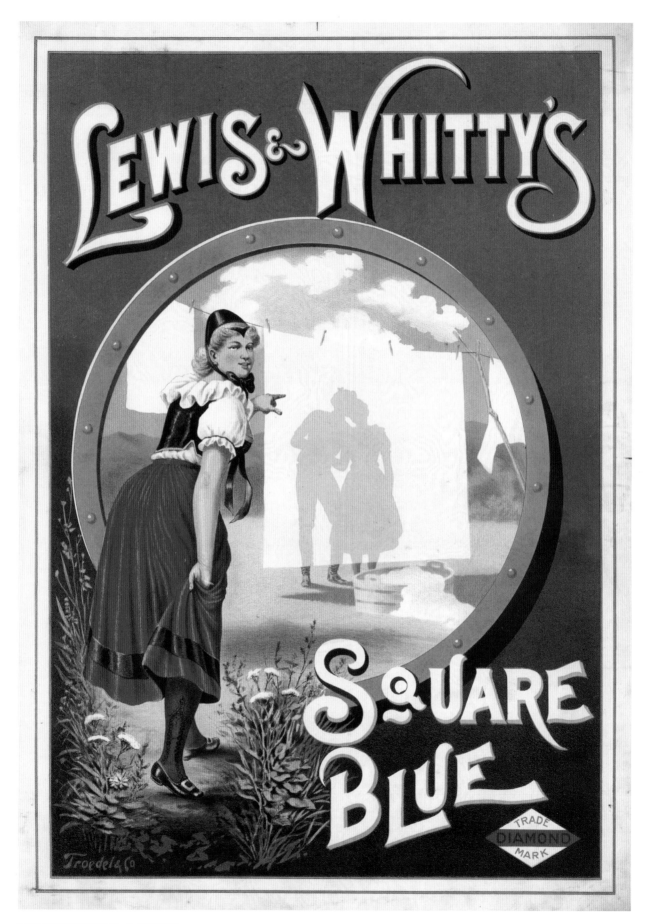

Lewis & Whitty's Square Blue (c 1881–1890)
State Library Victoria,
H2000.180/206

Lewis & Whitty's Vienna Washing Powder (1875)
State Library Victoria,
H96.160/2401

De Leon's Perfumed Carbolic Soap (1881) State Library Victoria, H96.160/315

diversified business, starting with boot blackening polish and leading to products including oatmeal, curry powder, sauces, washing and laundry soaps and starches.

In addition to the use of female imagery to attract custom, firms quickly saw an opportunity to expand their market and started to use images of playful, healthy and happy children and babies in their ads, to emphasise the importance of using the right product to secure the health and wellbeing of children through soap and bathing. So, while women were still the target market for the ads, they were not the focus of the illustrations. The use of well-groomed children played into the social status attached to cleanliness in the Victorian era.

In Victorian homes, cleanliness was a moral duty so '… creating a routine of regular bath time for the family was an expression of middle-class values: it was an effective way of promoting good health, cleanliness – and therefore respectability – and perhaps even, if the water was cold, character training.'[61] Having a clean, bathed and well-presented child meant presenting a heightened version of themselves and their family. The message was clear, and mothers were quick to believe it.

While changing living conditions and understandings about hygiene shifted public perceptions of cleanliness and hygiene and the importance of proper bathing and laundry, there was also a more important agenda at play in these advertising campaigns, with the rhetoric about health and hygiene used as a device to further colonialism and the civilising mission of the British. In the mid to late nineteenth century, the civilising mission of the British Empire sought to bring Western views of civilisation to what the British believed were the uncivilised corners of the world. These areas included Africa and Australia, as well as parts of Asia and the Americas. The idea behind the mission was simple and drew on Rudyard Kipling's 1899 poem, 'White Man's Burden', which exhorts the reader to embark on the enterprise of the Empire.[62]

According to 'White Man's Burden', in order for the world to progress, the white man (not woman) had to transport the uncivilised, darker skinned races into the modern era. Soap was critical in this regard. It was credited not only with bringing moral and economic salvation to Britain's 'great unwashed' but also embodied the imperial mission itself of washing away colour and otherness.[63] This was agonisingly evident in advertising for soap.

These advertisements, which drew on racial stereotypes and concepts of otherness, were designed to sell more than a product to the consumer. They were selling a set of ideas. That idea centred on the white race having a duty to civilise other 'lesser races'. By purchasing

De Leon's Toilet Soaps
(1881)
State Library Victoria,
H96.160/314

these products, the consumer is helping to bring civilisation across the globe, and these lesser races are grateful to the white man for bringing them civilisation.[64]

This notion is reflected in many of the early advertisements for soap products. One of the most notorious examples was an advertisement for N K Fairbank Company for Fairy Soap, showing a young white girl talking to a young black girl with the tagline: 'Why Doesn't Your Mamma Wash You with Fairy Soap?'[65] A & F Pears had a particularly regrettable track record in this regard. They produced an ad which was circulated during the 1890s which drew directly on Kipling's poem with the text reading: 'The first step towards lightening The White Man's Burden is through teaching the virtues of cleanliness. Pears' Soap is a potent factor in brightening the dark corners of the earth as civilization advances, while amongst the cultured of all nations it holds the highest place – it is the ideal toilet soap.'[66]

Another advertisement produced by A & F Pears, which has been the subject of several semiotic studies in recent years,[67] shows a white boy washing a young black boy in a bath, in two sequences.[68] In the first sequence, the white boy has a bar of soap in his hand, and the black boy sits in the tub awaiting his bath. In the second sequence, the black boy is sitting outside the tub, and has been washed white, his face aghast when

the white boy holds a mirror up against his still black face. The text across the top of the ad read 'For Improving the Complexion.' The illustration sequence and text convey the implied message that by using Pears Soap, your skin will be better, clearer, and whiter – and if you are black, your skin can be washed almost white.

Troedel's archive is unique in the conspicuous absence of similar images. Despite producing artwork for many of the big soap manufacturers, including A & F Pears, who had a history of using racist stereotypes in its advertising, this was not manifest in the works produced by Troedel & Co for those companies. That is not to say the Troedel archive is devoid of racist or inappropriate advertising prints. This much was apparent from some of the labels used and showcased elsewhere in this book. But when it came to soap specifically, these kinds of adverts were not part of the vast collection of prints the firm produced for soap products – a collection which stands in contrast to the broader history of advertising in the soap industry in the nineteenth and early twentieth century.

Kirks Fragrant Soap
(c 1881-1890)
State Library Victoria,
H2008.94/71

V
Fashion and Style

^
Advertisement Card for Hats
(1876)
State Library Victoria,
H96.160/1135

Advertisement Card for Hats
(1876)
State Library Victoria,
H96.160/2201

Today, women in advertising are depicted in various roles and with varying degrees of social status, ranging from the homemaker, business executive, sex object to superwoman. Before then, women got married, tended to the home and raised children. A woman's destiny was drawn upon by marketers and advertisers, and exploited at every opportunity, as evident in the advertisements for fashion and style in the Troedel archive.

The ideal consumer has always been female, and they remain so to this day. Early advertising practice helped define and shape the female consumer and the female identity, through stylised portrayals of female characters, objects, and images – contributing to the public understanding of gender roles and leaving a lasting legacy on advertising practice today.[1]

In the nineteenth century, advertisers were able to differentiate between men and women, and their respective marketing value. Men in the middle to upper-class households earned wages outside the home in the public sphere.[2] Women transformed those earnings into beautifully decorated homes, obedient children, attractive bodies and stylish outfits in the private sphere. This role expanded as the consumer economy expanded, and the needs of the household grew. Women took responsibility for these household needs and served as the household purchasing agent. Women, therefore, held all of the domestic power, and more importantly for advertisers, the power to purchase.

Literature and popular culture perpetuated the myth that the home was a sacred place where women cultivated a safe and nurturing environment for their family and intimate relationships. Publications warned against women leaving the home or having social aspirations. They also warned against the perils of being in the company of a man outside of marriage.

The Sydney Gazette & New South Wales Advertiser recounted one such disastrous narrative which ended in heartbreak and abandonment, and warned others against similar humiliation: '[o]ne of this unhappy class of females [who] occupies a little wretched hovel in my neighbourhood, and passes most of her time in lamenting the misfortune of having placed a generous confidence in a man, who, after an eleven years association, had inhumanly renounced her, at a period of life which leaves her hopeless of ever more enjoying the sweets of comfort.'[3]

These tales of caution were juxtaposed against those who preached about the personal reward and riches that came with romance and marriage. After all '... a women's wealth, social standing, home, and happiness, all came through marriage.'[4] While some women were consigned to the patriarchal marriage system out of a sense of religious or familial duty, marriage was welcomed by many women who saw it as a calculated mix of respect, mutual likening, social status and financial success.[5] We see this romantic idea of marriage and family, and women's role within it, in nineteenth century advertising, and especially for women's clothing, bridal wear and corsetry.

In Troedel's archive of advertising for clothing and apparel, advertising became more segmented and specifically directed at women. This targeting used traditional stereotypes in portraying the sexes, shaping society's understanding of what it meant to be masculine and feminine. Many fashion advertisements objectified and commodified the female body, and traded in helping women become more attractive to men.

So while the overt use of sex in advertising came several decades later, allusions to sex and sexuality were starting to surface in nineteenth century advertising. Societal attitudes towards this kind of advertising was mostly forgiving, and instead of impeding the growth of the industry, a local style scene began to materialise, supported by a thriving fashion trade, cementing Melbourne's status as the style capital of Australia.

The Wonderful "Wertheim"
Sewing Machine (c 1880)
State Library Victoria, Miscellaneous

THE WONDERFUL "WERTHEIM" SEWING MACHINE.

C. Troedel & C° Lith

TURN OVER

Crinolines, Corsets and Fashion's Greatest Fails

The Victorian period brought about dramatic changes in dress, assisted by the invention of the sewing machine by Thomas Saint in 1790.[6] The real game changer came with its mass-production by I M Singer & Co in 1851[7] (renamed the Singer Manufacturing Company in 1865), and its rivals including the Wertheim Sewing Machine Company, as advertised in *The Wonderful "Wertheim" Sewing Machine* (c 1880). Changes in the methods and technologies used to produce fabrics and synthetic dyes were also significant. These advances meant that clothing was produced quickly, and more cheaply than ever before, with garments increasingly made in factories and sold at fixed-price department stores. Print advertising and the proliferation of fashion magazines and European fashion plate periodicals such as *The World of Fashion and Continental Feuilletons*[8] and *The Ladies' Monthly Magazine*[9] appealed to the public to embrace these evolving trends, prompting a new age of fashion consumerism in the process.

Ladies fashion in the nineteenth century combined an eclectic mix of shapes and styles, including the neoclassical or empire style with its high-waisted, loose-fitting rectangular dresses that allowed for breasts to be prominently visible, the mutton sleeve, the bonnet, the large hat (adorned with feathers, stuffed animals, veils, and ribbons), bloomers, divided skirts, culottes and knickerbockers.[10] The most iconic part of nineteenth century fashion, however, was the silhouette, which was dominated by wide skirts, wasp waists and full-bodied bottoms. Crinolines, bustles and corsets were key to achieving this look. Advertisers immediately sought to sell these fashions and this idealised aesthetic to women, even though these undergarments provoked ridicule from the public, and forced danger and discomfort upon the wearer.

During the 1850s, skirts were the focus of attention. While full skirts were fashionable as far back as the fifteenth century, the bell-shaped profile grew in popularity during Victorian times, with skirts growing wider and wider. Decency and fashion dictated women wear multiple petticoats, even though layered petticoats were heavy and unbearable in the summer heat. As skirt styles expanded, these petticoats were also unable to bear the weight and maintain the structure of the fabric. And so, crinolines came to be.

The word crinoline is a combination of the French word 'crin' – a stiff material made using horse hair – and 'lin' – in reference to the linen used to make the original crinolines, although crinolines were also made of stiff fabric, metal and even wood. Some of the first crinolines were inflated, but they were so impractical they were soon replaced by the artificial cage crinoline, which was welcomed as a more practical alternative. These were made of spring steel hoops, increasing in diameter towards the bottom, and suspended on cotton tapes.

This design, which was the work of French designer R C Milliet, was strong enough to support the fabric of the skirt and create the desired bell-shaped effect. It was also innovative enough to be awarded a patent. Milliet's patent for 'une tournure de femme' was first granted in France on 24 April 1856 under the classification for haberdashery.[11] Patents were later taken out in Britain and the United States, with the crinoline described in the specification as a '... skeleton petticoat made of steel springs fastened to a tape'.[12]

Most men disliked the crinoline when it was first introduced, with some even swearing '... they would not marry a girl who wore one.'[13] Women were much more embracing. So much so that Milliet made 250,000 francs in the first five weeks of sale.[14] As a result, the crinoline quickly became mainstream, as women, and men became more accustomed to the look. The fashion became so prevalent that *Punch* nicknamed the crinoline craze 'Crinolineomania' – reporting that 'Crinolineomania may be said to be essentially a female complaint, although many of the other sex – husbands in particular – are continually complaining of it.'[15] Most complaints stemmed from the fact these cage-like structures were more foolish than fashionable. It cost five cents more to catch the omnibus in New York city for passengers wearing a crinoline. The rationale being that the crinoline took up the space that paying passengers could have otherwise occupied.

WINTER, 188

L. STEVENSON & SONS MELBOURN

LONDON

Troedel & Co. Lith. Melb.

Winter, 1886 (c 1886)
State Library Victoria,
Volume 20

Robertson & Moffat: Special Attention
Given to Wedding Orders (c 1880)
State Library Victoria,
Volume 20

The cage crinoline was awkward to wear, and hems could measure up to 33 feet round. To achieve the look, a woman's legs were encased in as much as 15 pounds of muslin, calico, flannel and horsehair, a condition that was hot and unhygienic. The crinoline was also cumbersome. Women had to master walking in them without damaging nearby objects. They also had to learn the art of sitting down without revealing their underclothes.

In addition to these frivolous complaints, crinolines were also deadly. Thousands of women died as a result of their hooped skirts catching fire, as they were constantly sweeping over open coals or flames.[16] Many more hoops got caught up in machinery, carriage wheels, gusts of wind or other obstacles, causing death or serious injury. In 1864, there were reports of 2,500 deaths in London alone from fire on account of the monstrous skirt, prompting the suggestion that '[a]t all events if crinoline must be the fashion then every lady should wear a fire screen or at least be attended by a maid with an extinguisher.'[17]

As the fashion for crinolines evolved, their shape changed. Instead of the large bell silhouette previously in vogue, they began to flatten out at the front and sides and increased in fullness at the back. One type of crinoline, the crinolette, created a shape very similar to the one produced by a bustle. Indeed, the crinoline was eventually replaced by the bustle from the middle of the 1860s. Bustles were similar to the crinoline in that they embodied a framework to create fullness and support excess drapery at the back of a woman's dress. They were worn under the back of the skirt, just below the waist, in order to lift the skirt off the ground and avoid dragging. For these reasons, bustles were an improvement on the petticoat and crinoline. They also held their shape, and would not flatten by the end of the day.

The bustle was on display in *Winter, 1886* (1886). This page is an extract from a fashion catalogue for Robertson & Moffat. The illustration depicts a scene of elegantly dressed ladies in an outdoor setting, standing on and around a Victorian style staircase and balustrading. The trees in the background are bare, alluding to the frigid temperatures, while the women are appropriately dressed for the cold conditions, in fur trimmed coats and feathered hats. Two young girls appear in the foreground, within arm's reach of their mothers. This scene plays into the advertising stereotype imposed upon female consumers today – where women are expected to play the role of dutiful mother and stylish fashion maven simultaneously. In fact, magazines and newspapers frequently offered up the archetypal modern women, celebrating her romantic and domestic roles, and the importance of consumption to the female identity.[18]

Robertson & Moffat commissioned Troedel & Co to produce many of its fashion catalogues and brochures. The firm was founded in 1852 and was based in Bourke Street in Melbourne, in premises that were later purchased by Sidney Myer and became the Myer department store in 1923. The retailer, who advertised themselves as general drapers, silk mercers, clothiers and outfitters,[19] provided dressmaking and tailoring services to their customers and held fashion parades in their showroom to promote new styles of dress and millinery imported from London and Paris.

Robertson & Moffat were known for their bridal wear, producing wedding dresses made of silk (damask, chiffon, taffeta, satin), lace and leather, and embellished with glass beads. Some of these are held on collection at the National Gallery of Victoria.[20] A sample of the style and silhouette of their bridal collection is shown in *Robertson & Moffat: Special Attention Given to Wedding Orders* (c 1880). Made to order, these dresses comprised layers of the finest fabrics, and decorated with intricate detail.

The styling of these fashion catalogues, and others from the same era, borrowed from the style and layout of the European fashion plate periodicals, which were heavily illustrated and printed using elaborate, high quality coloured plates. Indeed, the Troedel archive included some locally produced fashion periodicals, including *Craig Williamson & Thomas: Pictorial Book of Fashions* (c 1894), which was printed for Craig Williamson & Thomas, renowned Melbourne suppliers of drapery, woollens and clothing at warehouse prices.[21]

Fashion plates were typically produced through etching, engraving or lithography. They were coloured by hand and were considered to have a '... very high degree of aesthetic value.'[22] They were used by tailors, dressmakers and department stores to promote the latest fashions. Unlike fashion spreads today, the fashion of the day was not modelled by well-known celebrities or socialites. By contrast, fashion plates used generalised portraits, so the fashion took centre stage. These works often included descriptive text to accompany each look. Some of these sketches portrayed women with personality, where the models made eye contact to engage the viewer – a pose not commonly used in fashion illustrations produced during the nineteenth century.

These catalogues boldly showcased the bustle and the crinoline in all of its glory. As well as emphasising the full-bottomed skirts and bustles, these fashion catalogues also emphasised women and their drawn-in waist – a shape moulded by the corset. Compared to the crinoline and the bustle, the corset was a more enduring fashion staple.

The corset dates back several centuries in Europe and was historically worn by both men and women, to change and contort the appearance of their bodies. The corset became popular in sixteenth-century Europe, but reached its peak during Victorian times, when the corset became a mass-produced, factory-made commodity.

And although the corset has at times been worn as an outer-garment, as seen in the national dress of some European countries, it has typically been worn as an undergarment by women to emphasise the bust, waist and hips in a way to accentuate the differences between the male and female body. In this way, the corset is responsible for creating the public shape of the female body, which was widely popularised and promoted in nineteenth century advertising.

One of the more striking images in the Troedel catalogue was for the E.E.E branded corset. The poster was headed *The Celebrated E.E.E Corset* (c 1891-1900), and was 47.7 x 28.6 centimetre in size and printed on cream paper circa 1891-1900. The lithograph shows the female model wearing the French designed corset, with a crooked neck, critically observing the reflection of her impossibly thin waist in the mirror. Her face looks pained, a reminder of the price one pays for beauty. Corsets like this were sold in department stores, which brought factory produced fashion to the masses. Whole departments were dedicated to the corset, including in the newly established David Jones department store, whose corsetry department was '... very complete ...' with a range of imported styles to suit all body shapes.[23]

The corset was not just an object of fashion. It was political. Corsetry idealised the female form and cast female flesh into a shape and contour to be admired by men. The corset was also complete with contradictions. It was a tool used to contain female sexuality and express respectable femininity, and yet it also expressed sexuality by sexualising women's bodies for the male eye. The same can be said of the crinoline, as it produced a silhouette that was very attractive to men, by emphasising a woman's waist and large hips, while also preserving modesty, and demonstrating a

woman's delicacy, fragility and social status.

The relationship between the commodification of female sexuality and the marketing process is well established.[24] Some have even quipped that advertising is the second oldest profession and it arose directly out of the needs of the oldest – that being prostitution.[25] Indeed, '[t]here is scarcely a category in all of advertising ... that hasn't invoked sexual imagery, sexual situations, or just basic sex appeal.'[26] Central to the process of commodification was sexism and sexual objectification.

Sexism and sexual objectification go hand in hand with advertising and present a constant and ever growing problem in many countries.[27] The distinction between sexism and sexual objectification is nuanced, but there is a difference.[28] Sexism concerns distinctions which diminish or demean one sex in comparison with the other. Sexual objectification involves using women, mostly, as decorative or attention-getting objects, with little or no relevance to the product advertised.

While sex was not used as an overt marketing tool until the 1920s, there were allusions to sex and sexuality emerging in the latter decades of the nineteenth century in advertisements for fashion. This technique was largely accepted by the public, without question or concern. This included advertising ephemera produced by Troedel & Co. Richard Wendel's *The Ideal Velveteen Eclipses All Others* (c 1881-1890) provides a subtle but poignant example.

The 66.5 x 46.7 centimetre poster bears an image of two young women entwined, wearing Grecian style dresses, who appear to be dancing on air. The draping of fabric around the floating bodies borders on sensual – revealing the subtle contours of their curves while also alluding to the luxurious touch and feel of the fabric against the body. The royal blue backdrop is used to emphasise the point and further accentuate the themes of luxury and seduction.

The restrained colours and imagery used in this poster conceal the provocative, sexual undertones. That is what makes the image so salient. But more than that, the image also encapsulates how nineteenth century changes in fashion and style brought along with it a simultaneous change in the way the female body was displayed and perceived – emphasising the relationship between clothes and desire in a new way. This relationship, and the political nature of fashion was reinforced by the fight for property rights in fashion, and the curve of a woman's body with the invention of the corset.

Winter Fashions (c 1890)
State Library Victoria, Volume 20

Craig Williamson & Thomas:
Pictorial Book of Fashions
(c 1894)
State Library Victoria,
Volume 20

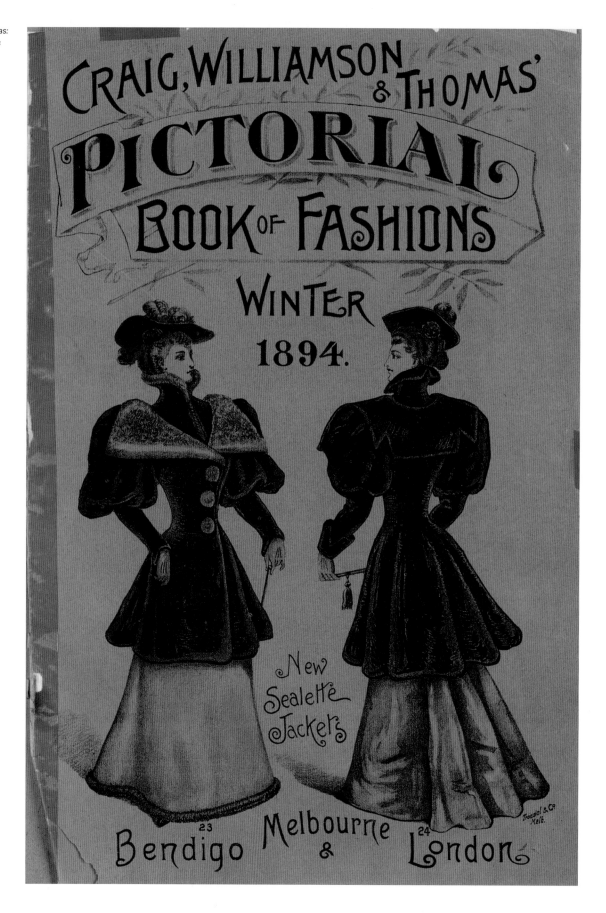

CRAIG, WILLIAMSON & THOMAS' PICTORIAL BOOK OF FASHIONS

WINTER 1894.

New Sealette Jackets

Bendigo Melbourne & London

Spring & Summer 1893-4:
Craig Williamson & Thomas
(1893)
State Library Victoria,
Volume 20

The Celebrated E.E.E Corset
(c 1891-1900)
State Library Victoria,
H2000.180/207

Patenting the Female Form

Women wore crinolines and corsets as part of their assigned ornamental role, adorning the home and society with their perfectly presented presence. The common thread binding crinolines and corsets was the way both garments constricted and constrained the female body into a romanticised, fictional form. Manufacturers sought to monopolise this through the patent system, patenting the female form in the process – and equating women's bodies to objects which could be bought and sold like property.

From the 1850s onwards, firms took out thousands of patents around the world for crinolines and corsets. The first crinoline patent was taken out in May 1856 by American W S Thomson in America.[29] Patents for improvements to the crinoline were abounding in the years to follow.[30] Thousands more were obtained for the corset. Up until this time, the patent system was dominated by men, with most applications lodged by male inventors. The avalanche of applications for corset patents changed this, and resulted in an increase in the number of female patent holders.[31] In fact, women obtained almost one-quarter of corset patents.[32] This is even though women lacked access to education, capital, business networks and sometimes, even the legal capacity to own inventions and enter into contracts to commercialise them.[33] The corset, therefore, was both a symbol of oppression and a vehicle for female emancipation, particularly for female inventors.

While female designers and inventors played an integral role in the history of the corset, the corset owes its existence to many inventors, both male and female, who patented improvements to its manufacture and who asserted their rights in the courts for many years.[34] These battles were not confined to claims about patent rights. As the branding associated with these patented corsets became central to the marketing campaigns of these manufacturers, firms fought fiercely to protect these additional elements of intellectual property. The result was a proliferation in litigation seeking to protect the brands and trade marks used to sell corsets in the 1890s, with many of these cases continuing into the next century.

One of the most protracted legal disputes in colonial Australia's history involved the corset. Front and centre were the Weingarten Brothers, and the patents and trade marks they claimed for their W B branded corsets. Weingarten Brothers was founded at the turn of the century in New York, manufacturing corsets which they sold around the world. In 1906, the *Sunday Times* remarked upon the magnitude of the trade carried on by Weingarten Brothers, who they described as '... manufacturers of the now world-famed W.B. corset ...' but whose fame had ascended '... by reason of big actions at law'.[35]

The firm first embarked upon '... its voyage through the law courts ...' when its rival, Charles Bayer and Co of London, infringed its patent by selling corsets bearing the W B label.[36] Having extended its successful business to the shores of Australia, Weingarten Brothers found itself embroiled in litigation again, albeit with mixed success. These cases arose out of the competition which had developed in the Australian market and included a continuation of the dispute initiated in England several years earlier between Weingarten Brothers and Pretty & Sons, which ran for almost three years and cost the parties almost €100,000.[37] In that case, the House of Lords found in favour of Weingarten Brothers, who were successful in obtaining an injunction against Pretty & Sons from selling corsets bearing the words 'Erect Form Corsets'.

The Australian incarnation of this dispute was the 1904 case of Re *Weingarten Brothers' Trade Mark*.[38] It involved an application for rectification brought by Pretty & Sons against Weingarten Brothers, whose ERECT FORM trade mark had itself been removed from the register in the previous year on the basis that it was descriptive (being an indication of the effect produced by wearing the corsets).[39] Weingarten Brothers had registered a trade mark in Victoria in 1901 consisting of the letters WB for use on its corsets. Pretty & Sons were also manufacturers of corsets and the registered proprietor in England of a trade mark consisting of the letters WB, which was used on its own and together with a diamond, to be applied to corsets.

Pretty & Sons had a long history of using the trade mark in England and in the United States of America. Upon discovering the Weingarten Brothers had registered its W B trade mark in Victoria, Pretty & Sons registered its own W B trade mark in Victoria in 1901 and the other Australian colonies in 1902. Later, Pretty & Sons Ltd filed a motion with the Full Court of the Supreme Court to have Weingarten Brothers' mark struck off. The Court held that if Weingarten Brothers' trade mark remained on the register, it might lead people to suppose that it had the exclusive right to the use of the letters.

Accordingly, an order for the removal of the Weingarten Brothers' trade mark was issued. Madden CJ noted by way of obiter that when Weingarten Brothers registered its trade mark they '… knew perfectly well that the applicant was entitled to a trade mark in England, which included these letters WB as part of it …' and Weingarten Brothers chose to take the risk and register the trade mark anyway.[40]

Despite the loss, several other cases were pending in different parts of the Commonwealth just a few years later in 1907.[41] At the same time, Weingarten Brothers had made clear its intention of issuing further proceedings in Western Australia, while also notifying the public that '[i]ts solicitors have been instructed to take action against any firm selling corsets branded "WB" which are not manufactured by the Weingartens.'[42] This included a case against G & R Wills Co Limited, which was later coined the 'Celebrated Corset Case'.[43] Weingarten Brothers were ultimately defeated, and it was held that the marks used by both parties were '… quite independent in origin, and there was no imputation of either party having borrowed from the other.'[44]

Way CJ heard the case in the South Australian Supreme Court, which involved a large cast of barristers and lawyers.[45] He complained about the duration of the court proceedings and the time it took for him to prepare his written judgment.[46] All in all, the hearing lasted 52 days and cost £20,000. It also took Way CJ almost four hours to deliver his judgment. Such was his frustration, that Way CJ referred to the case as 'abominable' in his private letters.[47] These comments and the long list of corset cases go to show that fashions may change, but the pursuit of fortune and fame is enduring.

>
Richard Wendel (1851-1926),
The Ideal Velveteen Eclipses All Others (c 1881-1890)
State Library Victoria,
H2000.180/224

New Shapes & Colors for Summer – Season 1898-9
(1898)
State Library Victoria,
H2000.180/226

The Style Capital

Nineteenth century fashion advertising was not just about undergarments. So even though women were an obvious target and feature of fashion advertising for crinolines and corsets, fashion and dress were promoted more broadly, extending to women's fashion in general, menswear and clothing for children. Troedel's archive is cast with hundreds of fashion ads and illustrations, providing a fascinating ethnographic insight into the Australian colonies, their people, and their place in the world.

Clothing carries an important aesthetic, social, economic and moral meaning, which is why people take fashion so seriously. Melbournians certainly did, setting the foundations for its reputation as Australia's style capital. Locals fared well in comparison to their European counterparts. Visitors even commented that those from the lower classes in Australia were better dressed than their English equivalents – and '[o]n hot days, the white dress, very generally worn by all classes, gives a lightness and gaiety to the streets, that is very striking.'[48]

Fashion was big business for traders in Melbourne, and a prosperous trade quickly arose. The arrival of the sewing machine was critical, speeding up the laborious process of manufacture and spawning a new local industry. As a result, fashion warehouses flourished in Melbourne (and also Sydney), and women flocked to these cities to work in garment factories in their quest for self-sufficiency. Reports boasted how these new warehouses could, thanks to the sewing machine, assemble a silk dress in just one hour and 13 minutes, a process that would have taken eight hours and 27 minutes by hand.[49]

Fast fashion came at a cost, however, namely for the women working in this industry, in the same way that it does today. Fashion commentators were alive to these issues, and they tried to educate the public accordingly. *The Argus* printed an exposé on the exploitation of female factory workers, reporting that: 'The good people of Ballarat have just become alive to the fact that the lot of the sewing girl, even in this protected colony, is not exactly a bed of roses, and they have assembled in public meeting to consider what can be done to ameliorate her condition.'[50]

Female factory workers were '... forced to attend at the workrooms we are told, at eight in the morning, and are not dismissed until midnight, and sometimes not until three o'clock the next morning.'[51] The young girls were often laid off at the end of their two year apprenticeship and were '... told that their services are no longer required, their places being filled up by new comers upon the same illiberal terms and conditions.'[52]

Despite ethical concerns about pay and conditions, the fashion trade in Australia endured, and prospered. The Australian fashion trade was heavily influenced by developments overseas, and fashionistas and traders looked to Europe for style inspiration. Fashion reports from Paris and elsewhere were filed in the local newspapers, with verses about muslin scarfs and black silk.[53] *The Argus* was very active on the topic and carried regular fashion reports. Many of these were filed for the different seasons, including a report on autumn fashions which provided detailed descriptions of dresses with Zouave jackets, flounces on thin dresses with wide ornamental sleeves and a cornflower blue barège.[54]

Most fashion columns were serious in tone, but some reports were much more humorous, borrowing from *Punch* and its satirical commentary on the day's favourite fashions. Again the crinoline was an easy target, with critics mocking the current day fashion in Australia and its seemingly implausible popularity. A report published in 1893 was especially derisive: 'I verily believe that fickle and frivolous dame, Fashion, is having a huge joke at present with ladies' dress. She wanted a change (it's good for trade, you know), and in looking over her old books to refresh her memory, being a bit out of sorts and temper, she lingered over those monstrosities of the crinoline period ... Thereupon that wicked autocrat selected all the ugly fashion-plates, and took a bit out of one and a bit out of another, and we have the most in-artistic and ugly fashion that ever existed! ... It is clever of Dame Fashion thus to heap assorted ugliness on the fair one's back; and we shall all, after this, welcome the much abused crinoline as a glad relief.'[55]

In addition to regular news reporting, a growing list of publications dedicated to fashion also surfaced. European fashion journals including *La Mode Illustée* and *Le Follet* landed in the colonies and were devoured by local devotees. These publications inspired the unveiling of a home-grown fashion journal – *Journal of Fashions* – which was launched in Melbourne in 1880 by Americans Oscar and Johanna Wigel. It included engravings and illustrations of the fashions in Europe. It also included patterns which were available for purchase.

Local retailers imported fashions and fabrics from Europe and advertised as much to emphasise the quality of their stock and catch the attention of those with a discerning eye for style. European fashion did not always translate to the Australian colonies. When it was realised that the Australian deference to European fashion was not appropriate for the colonial climate, a uniquely Australian fashion sense was born. The Australian heat was a compelling factor, with some calling for an 'entire revolution in dress' in response: 'The trying heat of a few days last week again forcibly reminds us that we are suffering from a too slavish adherence to British fashion. What is required is an entire revolution in dress. Dark, heavy-looking clothes are worn, tight-fitting collars, hard black hats, while black leather boxes, called boots, make up the robes of discomfort; and tiresome truckling to the dictates of "society" is the cause of it all. What in the name of common sense is the good of it?'[56]

A local style of dress did eventuate, but it drew heavily on the sensibilities of European dress. These local styles paralleled the radical changes in nineteenth century fashion, especially women's fashion, thanks to the mechanisation of dressmaking, but it extended to menswear and children's' clothing too. This included hats.

Hats were an accepted part of nineteenth century dress, and were worn to signal class and sophistication, by both men and women. Hats were worn as a mark of respectability. Even children were dressed in hats, as was customary at the time, with children overdressed and tidily presented. Hats were not just part of the established custom. In fact, hats took on an especial significance in Australia and became a necessary accessory to protect the skin from the sun.

Fabric was considered just as important as style in this local style revolution. Because of the peculiar Australian climate, there was a special focus on fabric, and its natural properties – that is whether it could retain heat, or allow heat to escape the body, to cater for Australia's cold winters and contrasting hot and humid summers. People were criticised for not taking these concerns seriously, and for not understanding the differences between fabrics.

Cotton and linen were highly regard, but wool was considered the most superior, and even though '... it cannot be made to look attractive or ornamental ... if it is simply a question of health VERSUS appearance, those who would sacrifice the former deserve to suffer.'[57] There is a beautiful irony in this statement, which is rooted in practicalities, being uttered in an era that was witness to the greatest fashion fails – the crinoline and the corset – both of which lacked any modicum of practicality. However, fashion never has been about practicality, and the masses continue to suffer for fashion.

Denton Hat Coy
(c 1880-1900)
State Library Victoria,
H2000.180/44

VI
Leisurely Pursuits

^
Richard Wendel (1851-1926),
*Dick. Comic Opera [at] Her Majesty's
Opera House Every Evening* (1887)
State Library Victoria,
H2000.180/72

The adoption of the eight-hour day in 1856 gave rise to a number of leisurely pursuits in colonial metropolitan cities. Melbournians especially took great pleasure in the novelty of dishing out their hard-earned spending money in public places during their leisure time. The struggle for the eight-hour day was long fought and hard won. The movement goes back to The Eight Hours League in Britain and the Trades Congress Union, who campaigned for eight hours of work, eight hours of rest, and eight hours of recreation and education.[1]

These justifications were central to the local movement. In Australia, the eight-hour day was a necessary reprieve for workers who had to endure Australia's harsh climate. Moreover, it was thought that men could be better husbands, fathers and make a greater contribution to society if they were given additional time away from work. The Victorian Operative Masons' Society noted in their 1884 report: 'The man whose mind is unclogged by the action and influence of severe bodily work, when in health will have his natural flow of animal spirits and kindred sympathies, inclining him to self respect, and respect for other, for law, order, and forms so essential to freedom, domestic virtues and good citizenship.'[2]

In Melbourne, the critical juncture came on 21 April 1856, after a group of stonemasons led by James Stephens, walked off the job at Melbourne University.[3] They were among the first in the world to achieve the eight-hour working day – and transformed the convict colony into the workers' paradise. The movement got traction thanks to the gold rush and the influx of labour, and therefore the idea spread across Australia to become one of the strongest trade union movements in the world. Of course, only a minority of workers won the eight-hour day initially. Chinese workers, Indigenous workers, women and children generally worked much longer, and for much less.[4]

Despite its limitations, the victory had a transformational effect on working families, granting working men more time off, away from work. Before long, this free time was consumed with new hobbies and interests, such as horse racing, competitive sports, ball games and other physical activities. *The Melbourne Sports Depot* (c 1885) illustrates some of these sporting interests and Melbourne's early obsession with sport. The 60.3 x 43.2 centimetre buff paper poster shows a young man in cricket flannels, holding a cricket bat, helping a young lady holding a tennis racquet and tennis shoes across a small waterfall in a recreation area. The poster advertises guns, bicycles, fishing tackle and other kinds of sporting equipment, toys and parlour games. Into the distance, two young boys are jostling with a football between two goal posts, while another two boys are further afield, wearing what appears to be their cricket whites.

Melbourne Sports Depot were also stockists of Coventry Machinists Co Club Bicycles and Tricycles. Coventry Machinists had a reputation which placed them on '... the most practical and, at the same time, most scientific footing.'[5] Their bicycles and tricycles were patented and of Royal patronage, with the Prince of Wales reported as using them.[6] Melbourne Sports Depot also '... received intelligence that ... the Coventry Machinists Company Limited ... supplied an "Imperial Club" tricycle to his Imperial Majesty the Czar of Russia for his amusement.'[7] Royal custom was a standard marketing tool, and allowed businesses to bring a certain level of esteem and class to their products.

Melbourne Sports Depot was located on Elizabeth Street. They moved to these premises in 1902, which were described as '... a magnificent addition to the street architecture of Melbourne.'[8] The building was designed by architect Nahum Barnet and built in two stages by Clements Langford for Frederick Dodge from 1902. Today, the building has been given heritage status by the National Trust '... for its notable decorative elements from Barnet's much-favoured tall-arch Romanesque revival phase, and for its contribution to the streetscape ... (and) ... historical significance as a remnant of Melbourne's foremost Edwardian sporting goods store.'[9]

Sporting equipment and other toys for playtime were a prominent fixture of the Foy & Gibson Christmas Toy Fair. The vibrancy of the event is conveyed in the poster *Foy & Gibson's Xmas Toy Fair & Magic Cave* (c 1881-1890). Foy and Gibson was one of Australia's earliest department stores and modelled on Le Bon Marché in Paris and other European and American stores of the period. The first store was 500,000 square feet in size and was established by Mark Foy as a drapery in Smith Street, Collingwood, in Melbourne. In the 1930s, the Orient Hotel on the corner of Swanston and Bourke Street Melbourne was demolished to make way for the city store. The business later expanded opening up across Australia, with stores in Brisbane, Adelaide and Perth.

>
*The Melbourne Sports
Depot* (c 1885)
State Library Victoria,
H2000.212/1

The store was known for manufacturing many of its own wares including manchester, clothing, toys, hardware, furniture and food and was eventually sold to David Jones in 1967. Foy & Gibson were also famous for its annual toy fairs, which boasted unprecedentedly low prices.[10] The fair was advertised heavily, and adults were implored to '… bring your little ones to see this enchanting spectacular.'[11] In its later years, the store attracted customers with its rooftop carnival, complete with ponies, train rides and a Ferris wheel.[12] Children could also meet Father Christmas, but it is unlikely he rode in on an emu, holding an Akubra hat, as he is in *Foy & Gibson's Xmas Toy Fair & Magic Cave* (c 1881-1890). The fun and frivolity of these toy fairs leaps off the page in this beautifully crafted poster, which captures everything that is unique about Christmas time in Australia – the heat, the dusty terrain and the native flora and fauna that make up the Australian landscape.

As well as playing games and sports and spending time at fairs in the great outdoors, Melbournians, or more precisely, men, also enjoyed the indoor facilities of newly built gymnasiums. One of the first gymnasiums to open in Melbourne was the Melbourne Athletic Club Gymnasium, as shown in *Melbourne Athletic Club Gymnasium* (1891). The members-only club offered daytime and evening classes for gymnastics, boxing, wrestling and fencing. The image shows the interior of the gymnasium located at 184 Exhibition Street, with men wrestling, weight-lifting, swinging clubs, riding a penny-farthing bicycle, fencing and practising gymnastics. Like most clubs at the time, the gymnasium was an all-male pursuit. Indeed, women were excluded from many social activities during this period, but there was one aspect of society where women played a pivotal role – the charity bazaar.

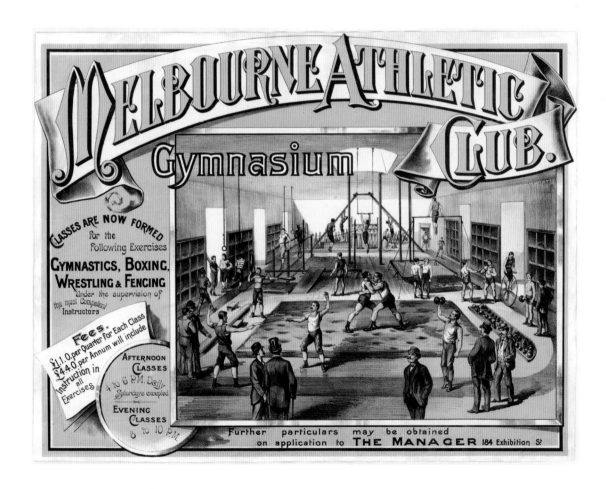

Richard Wendel (1851-1926), *Melbourne Athletic Club Gymnasium*
(c 1891)
State Library Victoria,
H2000.212/6

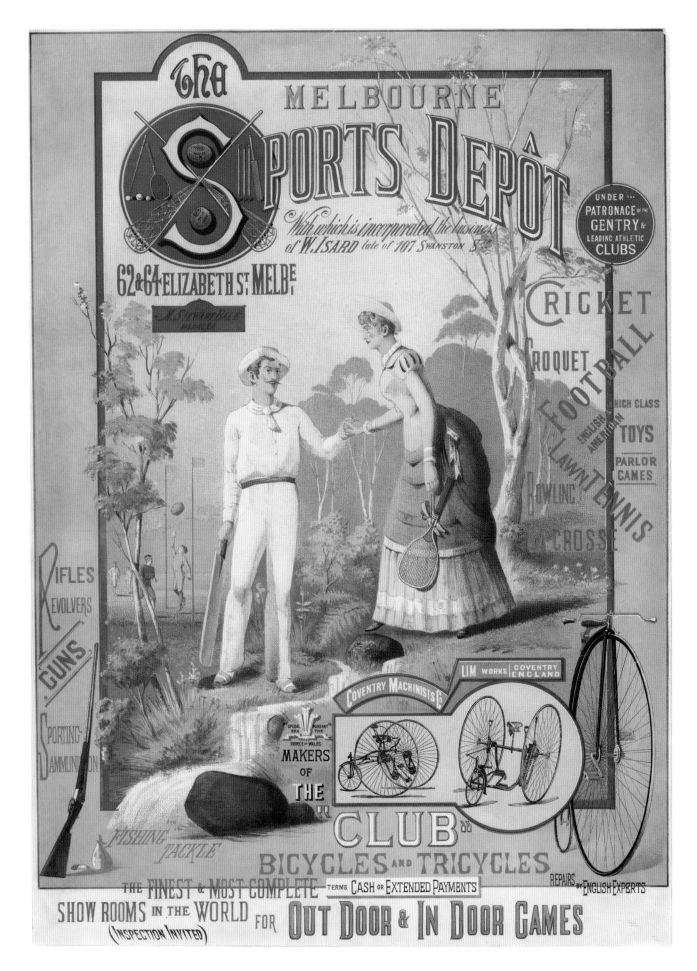

Foy & Gibson's Xmas Toy Fair & Magic Cave (c 1881–1890)
State Library Victoria,
H2008.94/19

'Crackerjack Cadet' Mouth Organ (c 1881-1890)
State Library Victoria,
H2008.94/65

*Abel Webb Turf
Commission Agent*
(c 1881-1890)
State Library Victoria,
H2008.94/26

GRAND
OPERA
CARNIVAL
OPENING
CEREMONY
DECEMBER
4TH 1886.
BY HIS
EXCELLENCY
THE
GOVERNOR
UNDER THE
PATRONAGE
OF HIS
EXCELLENCY THE
GOVERNOR
AND LADY LOCH.
EXHIBITION BUILDING
R. Wendel
T.J. Connor
R.L. Ievers
Hony Secys
Troedel & Co. Lith
Melbourne

Charity Bazaars and Philanthropy

Charity bazaars were omnipresent in the nineteenth century, right across Australia. They played an integral part of Australia's social and philanthropic life, permeating the lives of innumerable people including the organisers, participants, attendees and the beneficiaries of these events.[13] Varying in size, complexity, focus and duration, charity bazaars in Australia had some distinctive traits. The primary purpose was to raise funds for a designated charity or cause. They were predominantly organised and run by women, reliant on volunteers and free labour, featured hand-made goods for sale (but later mass produced products), and offered a variety of goods and entertainment, held as a one off event, or on a regular basis.[14]

Charity bazaars were the domain of women, standing in direct contrast to the other nineteenth century leisurely pursuits, which were dominated by men. They were one of the few activities of the nineteenth century where women had a space carved out especially for them.[15] The bazaar allowed women to exercise their creative and organisational skills outside the domestic sphere, within a socially accepted and philanthropic endeavour.[16]

These events gave women an opportunity for social interaction and community engagement and played a significant role in empowering women and cementing their place and space in nineteenth century society. Charity bazaars '... enabled women to manipulate their circumstances and participate in commerce, the marketplace and public life within safe and socially acceptable confines'.[17] There were broader societal consequences too, where '[w]omen's role and dominance at bazaars destablised general relations as women were on prominent display, actively selling goods and engaging with the public while men were confined to the role of consumers.'[18]

Troedel & Co produced the promotional posters for several charity bazaars hosted in Melbourne during the 1880s. The Grand Opera Carnival, as depicted in *Grand Opera Carnival Opening Ceremony, December 4th 1886* (1886), was one such special event. There was much anticipation and excitement in the lead up to the opening night of the carnival, and that extended beyond Melbourne.[19] The event was hosted in keeping with the growing tradition of charity bazaars and fundraisers which had popped up around the country in major cities and centres. On this occasion, the Grand Opera Carnival was poised to collect the £3000 required to make up the total for the establishment of a Chair of Music at the University of Melbourne.[20]

This colour lithograph was produced on buff paper laid down on board. It was 66.4 x 49.4 centimetres in size and designed to showcase the opening ceremony for the upcoming event. The bazaar was opened by Lady Loch, whose name is engraved on the stone statue, which is the central focus of the illustration. The statue is surrounded by men and women dressed in costume and listening to the man sitting in the middle of the scene, playing the lute. The Exhibition Building, which hosted the event, is standing proudly in the background.

The Exhibition Building was a popular venue for the major fundraising bazaars held in Melbourne in the late nineteenth century and early twentieth century. Built during 1879 and 1880, it was designed for the Melbourne International Exhibition of 1880 but over the years hosted the International Fair (1883), Grand Opera Carnival (1886), the Centennial International Exhibition in 1888, St Patrick's Cathedral Fair (1894), Artists' Carnival (1895) and Grand Fancy Fete (1895), among a long list of others. The Exhibition Building also hosted several hospital bazaars, including for the adjacent St Vincent Hospital in 1889, which was established by the Sisters of Charity.

<
Richard Wendel (1851–1926),
Grand Opera Carnival Opening Ceremony, December 4th 1886 (1886)
State Library Victoria,
H2000.180/149

The Druids Friendly Society Limited also had a long history of charitable activities. The company which was formerly known as the United Ancient Order of Druids Friendly Society Limited, was founded in 1862. Druids hosted several hospital bazaars, including the Melbourne Hospital Bazaar, which was first held in 1869. Raffles were used as a way to raise funds during these events and prizes were typically handmade novelties produced by the women involved in the bazaar, to keep costs to a minimum.[21] The major prize at the Druids' Gala Bazaar as shown in *Druids' Bazaar & Raffle* (c 1880-1890) was a 22 carat gold statue of a druid, which was valued at £1,000 and certified by the Royal Mint. The bazaar was hosted over the Easter weekend to raise funds for local hospitals and charities and included 125 prizes valued at £1,500.

>
Druids' Bazaar & Raffle
(c 1880-1890)
State Library Victoria,
H2000.180/163

THE COLONEL

MR AND MRS FORRESTER.

LAMBERT STREYKE

MRS BLYTH AND THE COLONEL

BURNAND'S GRAND AESTHETIC COMEDY

Played by Royal Command

At Abergeldie Castle Octbr 4th

PRINCESS OF WALES   PRINCE OF WALES   THE QUEEN

Before Her Majesty the Queen
The Prince & Princess of Wales
& the Court.

LADY TOMKINS.

NELLIE
"LOOK HOW THEY MAKE
ME DRESS!!"

BASIL GIORGIONE.

The only Play witnessed by the Queen for upwards
of twenty Years

C. TROEDEL & Co LITH. MELBOURNE.

The Golden Age of Melbourne Theatre

Melbournians were very charitable in supporting the booming bazaar culture, and the thriving arts scene it brought with it, which included the theatre. The growing arts and leisure culture transformed the city and the Melbourne nightlife. *The Australasian* reported: 'Melbourne is practically given over to him on Saturday night, and with his family ... he fills its bright and busy streets almost to the exclusion of every other class. He crowds the theatres, he throngs the shops, he and his are legion in the cheap restaurants.'[22]

Troedel's archive includes many theatre posters and perfectly captures the golden age of theatre and the Troedel family's unique connection to it. The theatre posters in the archive show '... the beautiful variety of textures he achieved (which is particularly evident in the black and white examples) the lively use of colour and the intricacy of the many illustrations reproduced. The posters also have a vivacity and immediacy seldom excelled even with photography.'[23]

The collection, which includes a series of theatre programmes and tickets, is considered to be '... a priceless collection of graphic theatre art.'[24] The styling of Troedel's theatre posters mimicked that of the French *Belle Époque* in the 1890s and although there were glimpses of this style found elsewhere in the Troedel archive, it was not as prominent and flagrant as it was in the collection on theatre posters.

The latter part of the nineteenth century marked the pinnacle of the French poster movement, with names like Pierre Bonnard, Edouard Vuillard and Henri Toulouse-Lautrec elevating the status of the advertising poster – which came to be considered highly original masterpieces, as they are today. Henri Toulouse-Lautrec's background is fascinating, with his first poster hitting the streets of Paris in 1891. He was physically disabled but artistically gifted, finding fame on a steady diet of absinthe and women, which ultimately led to his early death caused by alcoholism and syphilis at the age of 36.[25]

Jules Chéret was another master of the *Belle Époque* and is considered by many to be the father of the French poster movement. After being trained in lithography in London from 1859 to 1866, Chéret returned to France where he began producing posters for cabarets, music halls and theatres including the Eldorado, the Folies Bergère, Théâtre de l'Opéra, the Alcazar d'Été and the Moulin Rouge. His growing popularity saw him start making advertisements for the plays of touring troupes, municipal festivals, and then for beverages and liquors, perfumes, soaps, cosmetics and pharmaceutical products. He also created posters and illustrations for the satirical weekly *Le Courrier Français*.

The 1890s were a high point in the history of lithography and Paris was experiencing a surge in artistic printmaking, challenging the *peintre-graveur* (painter/engraver) mentality which drew a distinction between printmakers who designed images with the primary purpose of producing a print, and those who copied and reproduced a composition by another. The former being artistic and the latter being non-artistic.[26] The French lithograph movement was also assisted by the rise of printers like Cotelle, who specialised not only in commercial production but in artistic collaboration.[27]

Another important dynamic in the poster art movement was the growing taste for Japanese prints. In 1884, Japanese art and aesthetic was '... in the process of revolutionizing the vision of the European peoples ... [bringing] a new sense of *color*, a new *decoratie system*, and, if you like, a poetic imagination in the invention of the *objet d'art*, which never existed even in the most perfect medieval or Renaissance pieces.'[28] The trigger point came in 1854 after a period of over 200 years of self-imposed isolation, when Japan was forced by the United States to open its borders to international trade. As Japanese artworks made their way into Europe and America, including woodblock prints, ceramics, lacquer and textiles, they started to influence the artists and designers, with the Japonisme movement giving rise to modern art.[29]

Troedel and his commissioned artists drew heavily on the flair of the poster art movement in producing theatre posters, bringing some of the

<
The Colonel. Burnand's Grand Aesthetic Comedy (1882)
State Library Victoria,
H2000.180/47

C. TROEDEL & Cº THEATRICAL DESIGNERS & LITHOGRAPHERS.

W. H. LEAKE as RICHARD III.

style and sophistication of the French bourgeois to the Australian colonies. During the 1890s, Troedel was responsible for most of Melbourne's theatrical printing, and this continued for many years.[30] There were other players in the business of theatre printing including J P Fawkner; J N Sayers; and Charlwood and Son, General Printers and Booksellers – but none were as noted or as prolific as Troedel.

Troedel & Co's domination of the theatre printing market reflects Troedel's personal passion for theatre. Troedel and his family were keen theatregoers, particularly Walter Troedel, Charles Troedel's eldest son. Walter was '… an exemplar of Edwardian urbanity …' and reputed to have been the most charismatic and handsome and best dressed man in Melbourne.[31] Walter was reportedly engaged in an animated exchange with Marie Lloyd (an English music hall singer, comedian and musical theatre actress) from the stage box on her opening night at Rickards' Old Opera House in Bourke Street.[32] After a stint in the Troedel Sydney office, Walter became the theatrical representative of the firm and was responsible for the production of most of Melbourne's theatrical printing.

The late nineteenth century was considered the golden age of theatre in Melbourne, particularly the years between 1870 until 1910. This era gathered momentum as the colony expanded and cultural interests widened. During this time '… the theatrical posters developed from a mere advertising medium into a minor art form.'[33]

Melbourne's rich theatre history started with the city's first theatre, the Pavilion in Bourke Street, next to the Eagle Tavern, although it was described as a primitive affair.[34] The first performance was on 21 February 1872, by which time it had been renamed the Theatre Royal. The Opera House opened the same year, on 28 August 1872 with a performance of London Assurance. The theatre had a dark history, including a shooting during a performance of Les Huguenots.

The violent incident was the result of a domestic dispute and a husband's jealous rage where '[i]t seems evident that Mrs. Greer and M. Soudry had been intimate, that the husband knew it, that he became frenzied when he found the two together, and tried to kill them both.'[35] A witness described the perpetrator, Mr Greer, as '… a very excitable person, and he indulged a good deal in drink.'[36] Controversy continued, and the theatre made headlines a few years later, when a

young painter, Robert M'Gregor, died after falling from a scaffold while doing works at the theatre.[37] Eventually, the Health Department ordered the theatre's demolition in 1900.[38]

The Opera House had a bustling program before its quick demise. One performance on the program was the F C Baurnand comedy The Colonel. The play was first performed in Melbourne at the Opera House on 8 April 1882. The opening night drew a crowd, in a comedy designed to satirise the modern aesthetic craze.[39] It received positive reviews, and it was predicted that the show would garner the same popularity and success that it has achieved in London.[40] The following year, George Darrell's The Naked Truth opened at the Opera House which was 'Received by the Most Brilliant and Enthusiastic Audience Assembled In the Theatre for Years.'[41]

The poster for The Colonel is shown in The Colonel. Burnand's Grand Aesthetic Comedy (1882). In this poster, the image is broken down into various parts, which correlate to various scenes from the production. This was a common styling technique for theatre posters, where the underlying narrative was depicted visually, giving the audience a sneak peek into the drama that awaited them via these graphical storyboards. Reference to previous productions and Royal audiences were another key component of these theatre posters and the marketing message they conveyed – an attempt to bridge the distance between European culture and society and the colonies.

<

Richard Wendel (1851-1926),
W.H. Leake as Richard III (1881)
State Library Victoria, H2000.180/61

The Master and his Apprentices

As well as showcasing the prevailing styles of the time, the collection of theatre posters highlight Troedel's proud history of employing young apprentices in his art department, whom he collaborated with to produce these outstanding specimens. The most famous name to appear on the Troedel wage book was Arthur Streeton. Streeton was apprenticed to Troedel when he was discovered by Tom Roberts and Frederick McCubbin and went on to make his name as part of the Australian impressionist movement and the Heidelberg School. While Streeton eventually had his indentures cancelled with the firm, he looked back on Troedel and his time with the firm with great affection.

Years after his time with Troedel, Walter Troedel wrote to Streeton, to congratulate him on his recent knighthood. In Streeton's response, in a letter dated 17 February 1937, he wrote: 'Thank you very much for your kind note of congratulation. The honour is for the art of Australia as well as for me. I have often thought of the original old firm of your Father's in Collins st., and how kind he was to me. I did my first two or three good pictures during Saturday afternoons and Sundays when I was one of the apprentices.'[42]

Another exceptional artist who was apprenticed to Troedel and listed in the wage book was William Blamire Young. Young went back to England and after a short period at Herkomer's Art School at Bushey, Hertfordshire, he became involved with the innovative poster work of the Beggarstaffs. He returned to Australia to work at the Austral Cycle Agency, where he held the position of Art Advertising Manager from 1897 to 1899.[43] During his time with the agency, he produced the art-deco inspired piece, *The Poster Maiden* (1897), collaborating with Troedel & Co once again. The poster advertises Swift's bicycles, showing cyclists on the field, but it is the striking Poster Maiden which takes the viewer's breath away. Young marked the print with his monograph – the letter 'Y' in a circle – which appears on the bottom left-hand side of the print.

It is clear Troedel understood the value of collaborating with first-class artists and lithographers, such as Streeton and Young. He also worked with Charles Turner. In this era, the practice of lithographic printers and artists was intimately linked, with the skill and merit of each contribution considered equal. Given this historical relationship, the distinction between fine art and commercial art seems artificial and in many ways regrettable.[44] This attitude was one of many challenges printmakers and artists using lithography faced over the years.

The widespread use of lithographs was at various times hampered by the trade unions, who sought to prevent artists from drawing directly on plates because to do so would require union labour. Lithography's progress was also hampered early on during the Napoleonic wars.[45] Debates as to the legitimacy of lithography, and lithographs as art, was also limiting. In particular, lithography was criticised for being low brow and vulgar. Some critics wrote about not allowing lithographs into the house on the basis that lithographs were cheap, crudely drawn and that lithographic reproductions degraded the quality of artistic expression.[46] These debates became more pronounced when the technology evolved from black and white to colour, with concern raised as to whether these advances departed from the true essence of the lithograph.[47]

In time, and despite this negativity, lithography was embraced by artists, many of whom went on to build fruitful relationships with commercial printers. The history of lithography is witness to a long tradition of collaboration between artists and printers. Some artists produced prints for themselves, but often they lacked the same unique skill and craftsmanship of the professional lithographer, and so, their impressions were poorly inked and imperfect, necessitating a close partnership with a quality printer.

These collaborations were not without controversy. Divisions began to emerge between the artist and the printer, along with philosophical debates about what constitutes an original work for attribution and authorship. Ernst Ludwig Kirchner,

<

William Blamire Young
(1862-193), *The Poster-Maiden* (c 1897)
State Library Victoria, H2000.180/225

a lithographer from the early twentieth century, believed that '[o]nly if the artist really does the printing himself does the work deserve to be called an original print.'[48]

As to the individual printer, some believed that the artist (responsible for drawing the image to be printed) was superior, and the printer had a purely mechanical role and was lacking in intellect, imagination, skill or creative purpose. These classifications were drawn from the Victorian era class systems and the division of labour and status that emerged between the 'artesian' and the 'mechanical'.[49] Accordingly, '… while in this romantic scenario the artist was cast as creator, the printer was relegated to the position of a craftsman or artesian who looked after the allegedly "mechanical" tasks with his hands rather than his brain.'[50] As a consequence, and in drawing these distinctions and separating the mind from the hand, the true extent to which the printer was capable of contributing to the aesthetic of the final result was concealed and the printer's inventive, creative or interpretative contribution tended to be downgraded.[51]

Not everyone agreed with this categorisation or drew such sharp demarcations between the role of the artist and the printer. The father of lithography, Alois Senefelder always envisaged and considered their roles as equals, as artists. On this he wrote: ' … one of the most essential imperfections of Lithography, that the beauty and quantity of the impressions, in a great measure, depend on the skill and assiduity of the printer. A good press likewise is an essential requisite; but an awkward printer, even with the best press, will produce nothing but spoiled impressions. Till [sic] the voluntary action of the human hand is no longer necessary, and till [sic] the impression can be produced wholly by good machinery, I shall not believe that the art of lithography has approached its highest perfection.'[52]

In this way, particularly in the early period when the technology had not fully developed, the role of the artist and the printer were inextricably connected. And it was acknowledged that an artist could not be confined to their skill in drawing – they also needed some understanding of the lithographic printing process to foresee possible distortions and in order to obtain pristine impressions. So, while the art of lithography needed a talented artist to produce the original drawing, it also demanded an intelligent and highly skilled printer, who carried similar artistic qualities.

This was the view held by Raucourt de Charleville who wrote: 'A lithographic printer is a real artist and all the impressions he produces bear the stamp of his degree of talent; when he has wetted his stone, and has got his roller in his hands, he may be compared to the artist who is giving the last finishing touch to an Indian ink, or a Seppia drawing, like an painter, the printer must study the effect of his drawings, and distribute ink accordingly.'[53] In some instances, many lithographs were actually drawn on the stone or plate by the lithographer and not the artist, although the artist was consulted for guidance and approval and their prints were used as a template. This was the kind of relationship Troedel had with Richard Wendel.

Wendel was Troedel's most long-standing, and closest collaborator, and perhaps the most gifted. He produced many of the posters in the Troedel Collection, as well as the chromolithographs for the 'New South Wales Album' and the magnificent colour plates, many from drawings by Baldwin Spencer, which illustrate the zoological and anthropological volumes of Spencer's *Report on the Work of the Horn Scientific Expedition to Central Australia*, which was published in 1896. Wendel was an outstanding lithographic artist and draftsman. He came to Australia with Troedel in 1860 and together, the pair worked for Schuhkrafft for three years. When Troedel set up his own business in 1863, their association continued.

Wendel was born in Koenigsburg, East Prussia on 2 September 1851 and died on 26 July 1926. He was employed by Troedel & Co, as a principal artist, creating hundreds of posters and several more commercial labels and other ephemera, many of which have been catalogued throughout this book. Wendel worked for Troedel until around 1888, when he set up his own business on Collins Street, before leaving Australia for the United States and Europe, where he eventually died.

Most of the posters attributed to Wendel in Troedel's collection were produced as part of the theatrical arm of the business. The colour and vivacity used in these posters is second to none and showcased the full potential of lithography and chromolithography. Some of the more striking examples are shown here for *Jack Sheppard [at the] Criterion Theatre Commencing Boxing Night* (c 1886), *On Change* (c 1885-1890) and *Professor Perron. Eldorado Entertainment. Miss Ada Fitzroy* (c 1881-1890).

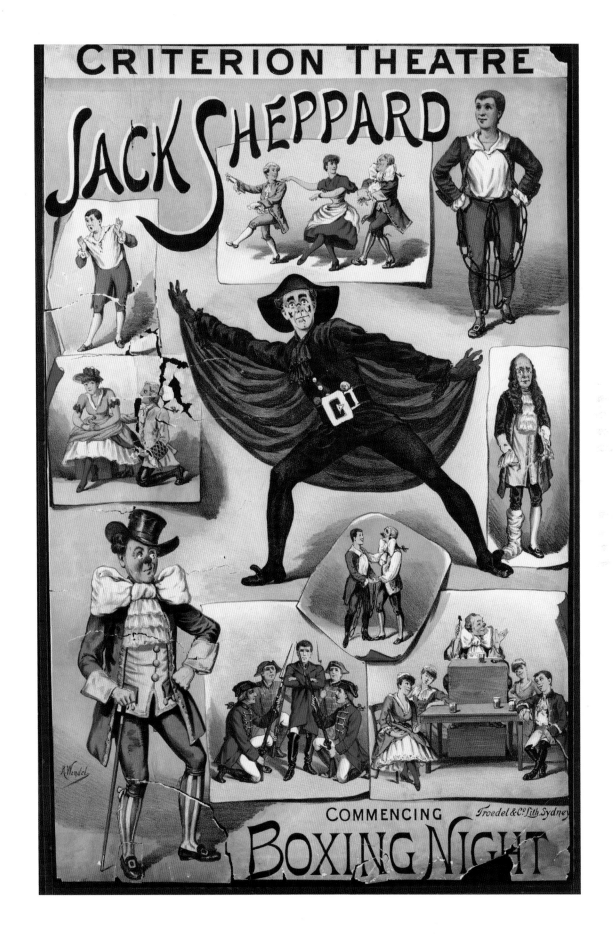

Richard Wendel (1851-1926),
Jack Sheppard [at the] Criterion Theatre Commencing Boxing Night (c 1886)
State Library Victoria, H2000.180/69

THE MAJERONIS IN "OII

N ELIZABETH"

Richard Wendel (1851-1926),
*The Majeronis in
"Queen Elizabeth"* (1886)
State Library Victoria,
H2000.180/65

On Change (c 1885-1890) shows an image of Rignold in costume as Colonel Challice, with a grey moustache, whiskers and eyebrows, staring out of the picture plane. Wendel engraved his signature, and the caption 'The Professor' at the forefront of the poster. The chalk lithograph was printed on cream paper and was 71.3 x 47.6 centimetres in size. *Professor Perron. Eldorado Entertainment. Miss Ada Fitzroy* (c 1881-1890) was printed in a similar style on white paper and included Wendel's signature. The poster shares scenes of the play. The central image shows Professor Perron on stage with his props, holding his magic wand. Four other small images show Miss Ada Fitzroy in her role as his assistant.

Another poster drawn by Wendel was *"Bad Lads" [a] Comedy Farce* (c 1881-1890). *Bad Lads* was the inaugural production of the new Alexandra Theatre which premiered in Melbourne on 1 October 1886. The theatre had been named Alexandra, after the then Princess of Wales but later became Her Majesty's Theatre. The poster shows scenes from the play, which was a comedy about married men trying to recapture the fun and freedom of their bachelor days. The poster was a chalk lithograph with tint stone on cream paper and was 50.5 x 71.4 centimetres in size. Wendel signed his name in the stone, as was his practice. The scenes from the play are accompanied by text below. The central image shows a restaurant interior, with two clowns emerging from under the tablecloths of two tables set with food.

The opening night was celebrated as a milestone in Melbourne's young but magnificent theatre tradition. The city had opened its first theatre 41 years earlier, and the Alexandra was being celebrated as the thirteenth theatre to open to the public in the city.[54] There was an overflowing attendance to witness the first performance, which was a '... distinct success ... that brought an almost continuous merriment to the audience throughout the show'.[55]

Jules Francois de Sales Joubert, the property developer who built the new theatre, hit a number of snags in bringing his theatre dreams to fruition. The building came in at £15,000 over budget when it opened on 1 October 1886. Joubert had hoped to open with a season of Italian opera but instead had to proceed with the low-brow comedy *Bad Lads*. Within a year, Joubert became insolvent, resuming his earlier career organising exhibitions.[56]

The poster *Bachelors [at the] Criterion Theatre Every Evening* (c 1881-1890) was produced at around the same time as *"Bad Lads" [a] Comedy Farce* (c 1881-1890) using the same technique – a chalk lithograph with tint stone on cream paper which was 71.1 x 50.1 centimetres in size. The poster also presented a series of small images with scenes from the play, arranged around a central image showing the characters seated in a garden. The show was playing at the Criterion Theatre, which was built in 1886 by architect George R Johnson on the corner of Pitt and Park streets in Sydney. The 'Cri' as it was affectionately known, was Sydney's most famous intimate playhouse at the time, until its closure in 1934. This poster was produced out of Troedel's Sydney office for the short period that business endured, as headed up by Walter Troedel.

Bachelors played for a short period and '... after keeping the audience in roars of laughter for a fortnight ...' it closed on 10 May 1888.[57] During the short season, the show packed out the theatre, and '[t]he comic situations which abound in this intensely humorous play afforded the audience great merriment.'[58] The production shared the same story arc as *Bad Lads* – men behaving badly. In its review, the *Sydney Morning Herald* wrote: 'The chief old bachelor – the cynical Marmoles, Q.C. – as well as the much-engaged Mr. Bromley, caused peals of laughter through the house. The "kissing scene", perhaps, more than any other, was the favourite with the public, as the comicality of the situation for all parties concerned is unsurpassed by any other.'[59]

<

Richard Wendel (1851-1926),
On Change (c 1885-1890)
State Library Victoria, H2000.180/2

"Dont go without me"

COMEDY FARCE

"Oh this is pleasure!"

BAD LA

BY
W. S. CRAVEN
AUTHOR
OF "MIXED."

"How lonely we shall be without you."

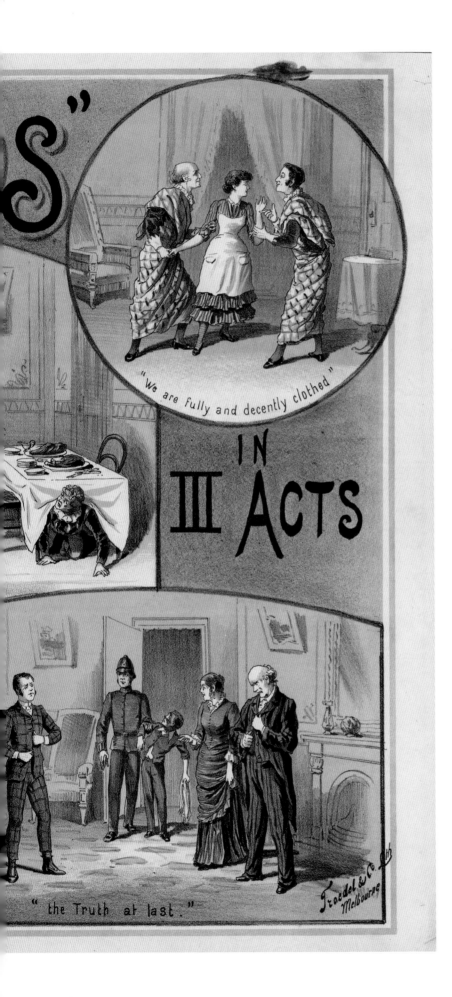

Richard Wendel (1851-1926),
"Bad Lads" [a] Comedy Farce
(c 1881-1890)
State Library Victoria,
H2000.180/74

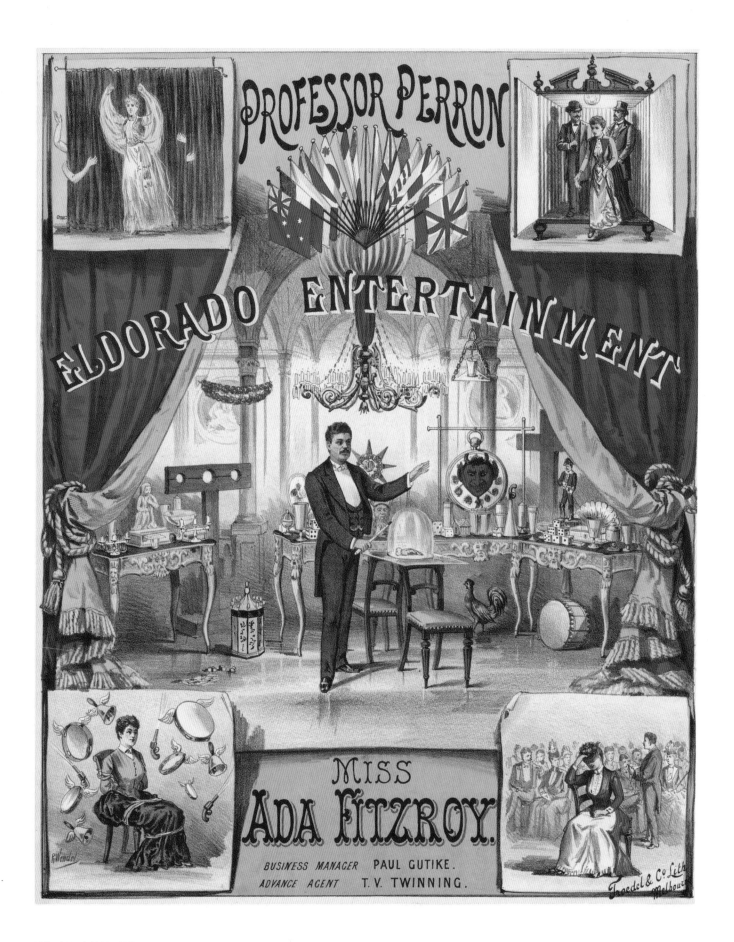

Richard Wendel (1851-1926),
Professor Perron. Eldorado Entertainment. Miss Ada Fitzroy
(c 1881-1890)
State Library Victoria, H2000.180/76

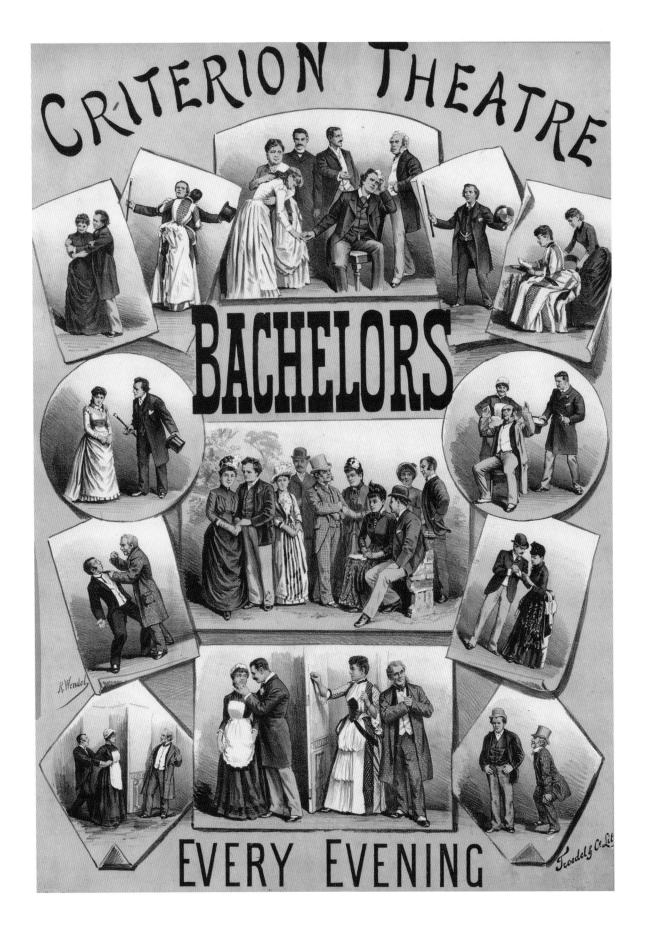

Richard Wendel (1851-1926), *Bachelors [at the] Criterion*
Theatre Every Evening
(c 1881-1890)
State Library Victoria,
H2000.180/73

Conclusion

1. 1st Life Guards.   2. 2nd Life Guards.   3. 21st (Empress of India's) Lancers.   4. Horse Guards (Blue).   5. 7th (Queen's Own) Hussars.   6. King's Dragoon Guards.   7. Duke of Connaught Bengal Lancers.   8. 1st Bengal Cavalry.   9. The Viceroy's Body Guard.   10. Royal Horse Artillery.   11. Royal Engineers.   12. Queen's Royal West Surrey.
13. Royal Field Artillery.   14. Highland (Black Watch) Piper.   15. Royal Welsh Fusiliers.   16. Northumberland Fusiliers.   17. Duke of Cornwall's Light Infantry.   18. Somersetshire Light Infantry.   19. Royal Engineers (Balloon and Telegraph).   20. East Kent (Buffs).   21. King's Own Rifle Corps.   22. Scottish Rifles (Cameronians).
23. Highland Light Infantry.   24. Cameron Highlanders (Queen's Own).   25. Black Watch.   26. Grenadier Guards.   27. Royal Irish Rifles.   28. Coldstream Guards.   29. Seaforth Highlanders.   30. Army Service Corps.   31. 1st Middlesex Rifles (Victoria and St. George's).

THE GUARD OF HONOUR.

REPRESENTING THE BRITISH ARMY AT THE AUSTRALIAN COMMONWEALTH INAUGURATION, 1st JANUARY, 1901.

^
The Guard of Honour.
Representing the British
Army at the Australian
Commonwealth
Inauguration, 1st January,
1901 (1901)
State Library Victoria,
H2009.115/7

Our fine arts were developed, their types and uses were established, in times very different from the present, by men whose power of action upon things was insignificant in comparison with ours. But the amazing growth of our techniques, the adaptability and precision they have attained, the ideas and habits they are creating, make it a certainty that profound changes are impending in the ancient craft of the Beautiful. In all the arts there is a physical component which can no longer be considered or treated as it used to be, which cannot remain unaffected by our modern knowledge and power. For the last twenty years neither matter nor space nor time has been what it was from time immemorial. We must expect great innovations to transform the entire technique of the arts, thereby affecting artistic invention itself and perhaps even bringing about an amazing change in our very notion of art.

Paul Valéry, 'The Conquest of Ubiquity', in Jackson Matthews (ed)
The Collected Works of Paul Valéry, Aesthetics
(Ralph Manheim trans, Pantheon Books, 1964) 225

Paul Valéry, French poet, philosopher and essayist, wrote this statement in 1928, anticipating the modern internet age and the torrent of media and reproductive technologies that would come to envelop us in the twentieth century and beyond. Valéry could have equally written these words a century earlier, in anticipation of the powerful impact that lithography would have on artistic technique and our understanding of art and advertising.

Lithography challenged the status quo, and so it took some decades for the process to flourish. When industry, artists and government eventually embraced lithography, it quickly came to dominate graphic design, graphic arts and the advertising world. Lithography was cheap and durable. It was also a dramatic improvement on existing print processes, and the quality of the impressions produced was far superior to any existing means of print production. Above all, lithography promised prints for the masses and became a democratic art.[1] Even so, the virtues of lithography were hijacked by its detractors, who categorised these benefits as the technology's greatest flaws.

Lithographs were regarded as illegitimate when compared to other artistic mediums, including watercolour paintings, oil on canvas, and portraits. Critics objected to the mass reproduction of prints,

labelling lithographs as 'mere merchandise' and 'pseudo culture'.[2] In the early days, those working with lithographs were not treated as artists, as art involved the creative and the original. Instead, lithography was looked upon as a mere handicraft, and '... every painter, however eminent, ceases to be an artist, and becomes a mere workman (more or less skilful) the very moment that he begins to copy one of his own pieces, or the pictures of any one else.'[3]

This sentiment was further expressed by Walter Benjamin, in his famous essay on the impact of modern technologies of reproduction, *The Work of Art in the Age of Mechanical Reproduction*.[4] Benjamin, who quoted Valéry in his opening paragraph, claimed that lithography (and photography and film) had broken the 'auratic' qualities of art and culture. Whereas early fine art maintained prestige through distance, embodied in unique objects set in particular locations of worship, modern reproduction brought art and culture into people's homes. Everyone could now have a copy of a masterpiece above the mantelpiece, and this intimacy ripped the auratic shroud off artistic consumption.

Thus, while some praised lithography as the principal means for developing a democratising art, others shuddered at the thought of these

176

prints passing for art by a large body of 'slenderly-equipped persons' with no sense of culture. These same critics believed mechanically reproduced information and images posed a threat to the legitimate reproduction of culture.[5] Chromolithographs and advertising posed an even greater threat to culture as they '... appealed to the lowest levels of taste in order to sell products ...'[6]

These debates tarnished the lithograph to such an extent that they were not considered worthy of serious scholarly attention or discussion. Lithographs would never replace the original, this much was true. And yet – then, and now – people enjoy and appreciate reproductions of fine art. People also take pleasure in collecting advertising lithographs and poster art, today, more than ever.

The boundaries of the art world have become more porous, with the definition of art broad enough to encompass anything that evokes an aesthetic reaction, ranging from fine art to wild art.[7] So while lithography was dismissed by many people, for many years, with these works often diminished as nostalgia labels or kitsch carrying little meaning and value – more than one hundred and fifty years later – the true value of the lithograph is finally being realised. The result is a growing body of work devoted to unearthing libraries of lost lithographs.[8] This book, and its focus on the Troedel archive adds to this movement.

Troedel, and the talented artists he worked with produced some of the most technically accomplished prints produced in that period, rivalling works produced on canvas. This compilation left a lasting impression of early colonial life, an impression that has been buried in the State Library of Victoria, unexamined and overlooked, until now. This amazing archive provides a vivid, graphic history of nineteenth century Australia, providing a capsule collection of Australia's colonial heritage, where art, advertising and the law intersect.

These illustrations were conceptually complex and challenging, covering a diverse range of themes, from the frivolous to the sensitive and the serious. The archive showcases the glamorisation of alcohol and cigarettes, the commodification of women in advertising for the sake of fashion and the male gaze, as well as the targeting of vulnerable customers with magic pills and unproven remedies. It also includes the commodification of indigenous culture, and the use of stereotypes to entrench existing power structures and disempower the other. The collection of theatre posters bear depictions of men behaving badly in sell-out stage performances, without challenge or repercussion.

There is a startling familiarity to these themes. On the one hand, Troedel's lithographs represent a period of intense transformation in advertising aesthetic and practice. At the same time, these prints are prophetic of what was to come in the next century of advertising – in print, and across the new mediums of communication. This book, therefore, is as much a *preface* of Australian advertising, as it is a *history* – a history printed on stone.

Richard Wendel (1851-1926),
First Arrival New Season Teas
1888-9 (1888)
State Library Victoria, H2000.180/108

‘The Melbourne Album’

‘The Melbourne Album’

Charles Troedel (1836-1906)
'The Melbourne Album', by the lithographer and
publisher Charles Troedel, Melbourne (1864)
State Library Victoria, 30328102131686/1 (title page)

The Melbourne Album

Containing a Series of Views of
Melbourne & Country Districts.

Respectfully dedicated to, and Patronized by His Excellency
Sir Charles Darling K.C.B.

BY THE
Lithographer and Publisher,
CHARLES TROEDEL.
73, Collins St.E. Melbourne.

François Cogné (1829-1883),
Botanical Gardens (1863)
Published by Charles Troedel, at the Melbourne
Album Office, 73 Collins Street East, Melbourne
State Library Victoria, 30328102131686/2, Plate 1

BOTANICAL GARDENS

François Cogné (1829-1883),
Collins Street (1863)
Published by Charles Troedel at Schuhkrafft's
178 Elizabeth Street, Melbourne
State Library Victoria, 30328102131686/3, Plate 2

François Cogné (1829-1883),
Dight's Mill (1863)
Published by Charles Troedel at Schuhkrafft's 178
Elizabeth Street, Melbourne
State Library Victoria, 30328102131686/4, Plate 3

François Cogné (1829-1883),
Bourke Street (1863)
Published by Charles Troedel, at the Melbourne
Album Office, 73 Collins Street East, Melbourne
State Library Victoria, 30328102131686/5, Plate 4

François Cogné (1829-1883),
Fitzroy Gardens (1863)
Published by Charles Troedel, at the Melbourne
Album Office, 73 Collins Street East, Melbourne
State Library Victoria, 30328102131686/6, Plate 5

FITZROY GARDENS

François Cogné (1829-1883),
Swanston Street (1863)
Published by Charles Troedel, at the Melbourne
Album Office, 73 Collins Street East, Melbourne
State Library Victoria, 30328102131686/7, Plate 6

François Cogné (1829-1883),
Sheepwash Creek (1863)
Published by Charles Troedel, at the Melbourne
Album Office, 73 Collins Street East, Melbourne
State Library Victoria, 30328102131686/8, Plate 7

François Cogné (1829-1883),
Treasury Buildings (1863)
Published by Charles Troedel, at the Melbourne
Album Office, 73 Collins Street East, Melbourne
State Library Victoria, 30328102131686/9, Plate 8

François Cogné (1829-1883),
The Lal Lal Falls (1863)
Published by Charles Troedel, at the Melbourne
Album Office, 73 Collins Street East, Melbourne
State Library Victoria, 30328102131686/10, Plate 9

THE LAL LAL FALLS

NEAR BALLARAT. (1863)

Published at the Melbourne Album Office, 73, Collins S.t East.

François Cogné (1829–1883),
Sandridge (1863)
Published by Charles Troedel, at the Melbourne
Album Office, 73 Collins Street East, Melbourne
State Library Victoria, 30328102131686/11, Plate 10

Melbourne Cricket Ground (1864)
Published by Charles Troedel, at the Melbourne
Album Office, 73 Collins Street East, Melbourne
State Library Victoria, 30328102131686/12, Plate 11

MELBOURNE CRICKET GROUND

François Cogné (1829-1883),
Great Lonsdale Street East (1864)
Published by Charles Troedel, at the Melbourne
Album Office, 73 Collins Street East, Melbourne
State Library Victoria, 30328102131686/13, Plate 12

GREAT LONSDALE STREET EAST
(1864)

Published by Charles Troedel, Melbourne Album Office 73, Collins St East

Merry Creek (1864)
Published by Charles Troedel, at the Melbourne
Album Office, 73 Collins Street East, Melbourne
State Library Victoria, 30328102131686/14, Plate 13

MERRY CREEK.
(PLENTY RANGES, 1864)

François Cogné (1829-1883),
Queens Wharf (1864)
Published by Charles Troedel, at the Melbourne
Album Office, 73 Collins Street East, Melbourne
State Library Victoria, 30328102131686/15, Plate 14

QUEENS WHARF.
(YARRA YARRA 1864.)

Published by Charles Troedel, Melbourne Album Office, 73 Collins St East

View from Studley Park (1864)
Published by Charles Troedel, at the Melbourne
Album Office, 73 Collins Street East, Melbourne
State Library Victoria, 30328102131686/16, Plate 15

VIEW FROM STUDLEY PARK.

Published by Charles Troedel, Melbourne Album Office, 73 Collins St. East.

Edward Gilks (c 1822-unknown),
Elizabeth Street (1864)
Published by Charles Troedel, at the Melbourne
Album Office, 73 Collins Street East, Melbourne
State Library Victoria, 30328102131686/17, Plate 16

ELIZABETH STREET

From an oil painting by E von Guérrard,
View on the Upper Mitta Mitta (1864)
Published by Charles Troedel, at the Melbourne
Album Office, 73 Collins Street East, Melbourne
State Library Victoria, 30328102131686/18, Plate 17

Edward Gilks (c 1822–unknown),
Flinders Street (1864)
Published by Charles Troedel, at the Melbourne
Album Office, 73 Collins Street East, Melbourne
State Library Victoria, 30328102131686/19, Plate 18

Frederick Schoenfeld (c 1810-1860),
View on Eastern Hill (1864)
Published by Charles Troedel, at the Melbourne
Album Office, 73 Collins Street East, Melbourne
State Library Victoria, 30328102131686/20, Plate 19

VIEW ON EASTERN HILL
FROM HALF WAY HOUSE ALBERT ST.
Printed & Published by Charles Troedel Melbourne Album Office, 73 Collins St East.

James Buckingham Philp (1830–unknown),
St Kilda (1864)
Published by Charles Troedel, at the Melbourne
Album Office, 73 Collins Street East, Melbourne
State Library Victoria, 30328102131686/21, Plate 20

Nicholas Chevalier (1828-1902),
Wenworth River Diggings (1864)
Published by Charles Troedel, at the Melbourne
Album Office, 73 Collins Street East, Melbourne
State Library Victoria, 30328102131686/22, Plate 21

WENTWORTH RIVER DIGGINGS
GIPPS LAND
From a Picture by N. Chevalier – Printed and Published by Charles Troedel, Melbourne Album Office, 73, Collins St East

James Buckingham Philp (1830-unknown),
The Eastern Market (1864)
Published by Charles Troedel, at the Melbourne
Album Office, 73 Collins Street East, Melbourne
State Library Victoria, 30328102131686/23, Plate 22

THE EASTERN MARKET
FROM TOP OF WHITTINGTON TAVERN
Printed and Published by Charles Troedel, Melbourne Album Office, 73 Collins Street, East

Nicholas Chevalier (1828-1902),
Mount Abrupt and the Grampians (1864)
Published by Charles Troedel, at the Melbourne
Album Office, 73 Collins Street East, Melbourne
State Library Victoria, 30328102131686/24, Plate 23

MOUNT ABRUPT and THE GRAMPIANS.

Nicholson Street (1864)
Published by Charles Troedel, at the Melbourne
Album Office, 73 Collins Street East, Melbourne
State Library Victoria, 30328102131686/25, Plate 24

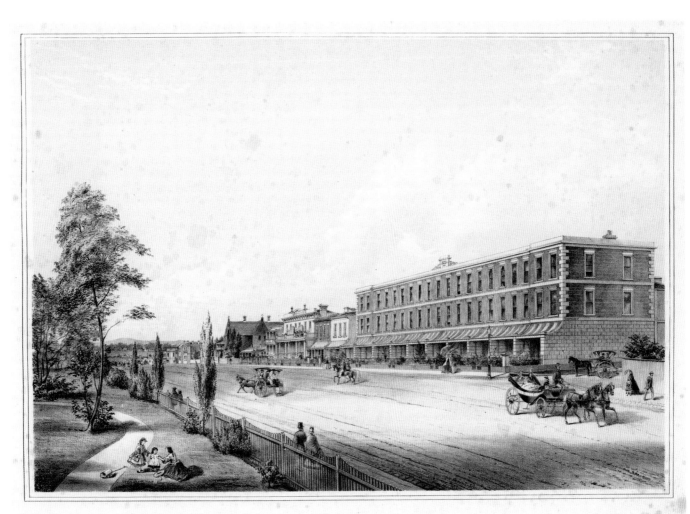

NICHOLSON STREET

Endnotes

Introduction

1. Phillip Vannini, *Material Culture and Technology in Everyday Life: Ethnographic Approaches* (Peter Lang, 2009) 3.

2. Ferdinand de Saussure, (1966), *A Course in General Linguistics* (W Baskin trans, McGraw-Hill, 1966). Also see Roland Barthes, *Writing Degree Zero and Elements of Semiology* (A Lavers & C Smith trans, Beacon, 1970) and Umberto Eco, *A Theory of Semiotics* (Indiana University Press, 1976).

3. For more on the use of objects as a way to compile a history on a discrete theme or concept see Claudy Op den Kamp and Dan Hunter (eds) *A History of IP in 50 Objects* (Oxford University Press, 2019).

4. R W Budd, R K Thorp and L Donohew, *Content Analysis of ommunications* (Macmillan, 1967). Also see Klaus Krippendorff, *Content Analysis: An Introduction to its Methodology* (Sage Publications, 2nd ed, 2004).

5. This is consistent with the way these tools are used by other scholars. See for example Bernard Berelson, *Content Analysis in Communication Research* (The Free Press, 1952).

6. Clive Turnbull (ed), 'The Melbourne Album': *Comprising a Series of Elegant, Tinted, Lithographic Views of Melbourne and Surrounding Districts Lithographed*, Printed and Published by Charles Troedel in 1863 (Georgian House, 1961). Also see *Nicholas Chevalier's Album of Chromo Lithographs* (1864-1865).

7. The archive includes the company's wage and salary books from 1904-1928, company ledgers from 1897-1933, and stock records from 1905-1915 and 1966-1967. The collection also includes a list of the firm's apprentices from 1890-1918. The archive further consists of examples of show cards, letterheads, share certificates, brightly coloured labels for food and drink products and posters showing theatrical productions, stage personalities, breweries, factories and land sales. Finally, the archive includes some patent records and related orrespondence. For more see *Troedel Archive*, State Library Victoria <http://www.slv.vic.gov.au/search-discover/explore-collections-format/pictures/troedel-archive>.

8. 'Retirement Ends 65 Years' Printing', *The Age* (Melbourne), 26 April 1963, 4.

Chapter I: The Visual Century

1. 'Obituary: The Late Mr Charles Troedel', January 1907.

2. Ibid.

3. Ibid.

4. Troedel would have arrived in Australia on a Danish passport on account of the fact that before the Prussian War, residents who lived inside the walled city of Hamburg were called Hamburgers, while those who worked in Hamburg but lived outside the wall were considered Danish.

5. Clive Turnbull (ed), 'The Melbourne Album': *Comprising a Series of Elegant, Tinted, Lithographic Views of Melbourne and Surrounding Districts Lithographed, Printed and Published by Charles Troedel in 1863* (Georgian House, 1961) 9.

6. See, eg, 'City Fire: Troedel's Printing Works Gutted', T*he Australasia* (Melbourne), 13 February 1904, 29.

7. 'German Emigration', *Port Phillip Gazette & Settler's Journal* (Melbourne), 9 December 1846, 2.

8. 'The Vineyard: Introduction of Vine Grower's from the Continent', *The Farmer's Journal & Gardener's Chronicle* (Melbourne), 31 May 1862, 11.

9. Felicity Jensz, *German Moravian Missionaries in the British Colony of Victoria, Australia, 1848-1908: Influential Strangers* (Brill, 2010).

10. Origins: Immigrant Communities in Victoria, *History of Immigration from Germany* Museum Victoria <https://museumvictoria.com.au/origins/history.aspx?pid=22>.

11. The business did register some patents in the twentieth century relating to its print process. The patent records can be found in the State Library of Victoria. See *Troedel Archive*, State Library Victoria <http://www.slv.vic.gov.au/search-discover/explore-collections-format/pictures/troedel-archive>.

12. *The Argus* (Melbourne), 26 June 1869, 4.

13. *The Argus* (Melbourne), 11 September 1884, 5.

14. Ibid.

15. Although it was usually referred to as 'The Melbourne Album', the full title of the collection was 'The Melbourne Album', *Containing a Series of Views of Melbourne & Country Districts (Respectfully Dedicated to, and Patronized by His Excellency Sir Charles Darling, K.C.B).*

16. Turnbull, above n 5, 13.

17. 'New South Wales Album' (Charles Troedel & Co, 1878).

18. 'Publications and Literature', *The Argus* (Melbourne), 25 July 1863, 8.

19. Ibid.

20. Turnbull, above n 5, 33.

21. Ibid.

22. Victorian Heritage Database, *Dights Mill Site* (21 July 1999) Heritage Council Victoria <http://vhd.heritagecouncil.vic.gov.au/places/2>.

23. See Turnbull, above n 5. It has since been discovered that some of the textual matters included in this edition are factually inaccurate.

24. Harold Freedman, *The Book of Melbourne and Canberra: A Collection of Six Lithograph Prints of Melbourne Drawn in 1962-1963* (Griffin Press, 1966) 2.

25. Turnbull, above n 5, 11.

26. Ibid 10.

27. Clinton Adams, 'The Nature of Lithography' in Pat Gilmour (ed), *Lasting Impressions: Lithographs as Art* (Australian National Gallery, 1988) 25, 25.

28. Dennis Bryans, *A Seed of Consequence: Indirect Image Transfer and Chemical Printing: The Role Played by Lithography in the Development of Printing Technology* (PhD Thesis, Swinburne University of Technology, 2000) 3.

29. On the history of photography and the battle between the photograph and the subject see Jessica Lake, *The Face that Launched a Thousand Lawsuits: The American Women who Forged a Right to Privacy* (Yale University Press, 2016).

30. Scott McQuire, *Visions of Modernity* (Sage, 1997). Also see Jonathan Crary, T*echniques of the Observer* (MIT Press, 1990).

31. Alois Senefelder, *A Complete Course on Lithography* (A S trans, Ackermann, 1819) 9-10.

32. Ibid 32-3.

33. British Patent Number 2518 (20 June 1801).

34. Senefelder, above n 31.

35. Ibid 93.

36. Bryans, above n 28, 4.

37. Jean Gittins, *Osborne, John Walter (1828-1902)* Australian Dictionary of Biography <http://adb.anu.edu.au/biography/osborne-john-walter-4343>.

38. Senefelder, above n 31, 334-35.

39. In fact, Engelmann wrote about lithography having mastered monochrome lithography in Godefroy Engelmann, *Manuel du Dessinateur Lithographe* (Chez l'auteur, 1822). He later won a competition announced by *La Société d'Encouragement pour l'Industrie National* (The Society for Encouraging National Industry) for his tri-colour printing method in 1939, even though he was reportedly awarded a patent for his process in 1837, although the patent number is unknown.

40. On the development of typeface and fonts in the eighteenth century see David Raizman, *History of Modern Design* (Prentice Hall, 2nd ed, 2011) 40-42.

41. Although it has been said of this period, '[m]ost chromos were gaudy and short-lived …' and were considered as mere paper ephemera. See Juliann Sivulka, *Soap, Sex, and Cigarettes: A Cultural History of American Advertising* (Cengage Learning, 2nd ed, 2012) 30.

42. See, eg, Michael Jubb, *Cocoa and Corsets: A Selection of Late Victorian and Edwardian Posters and Showcards from the Stationers' Company Copyright Records Presented in the Public Record Office* (Stationery Office Books, 1984) which presents a selection of posters and show cards from the Stationers' Company copyright records.

43. See *Paris Convention for the Protection of Industrial Property*, WO020EN (entered into force 20 March 1883).

44. In England, some patent claims purported to extend to 'His Majesty's Colonies and Plantations Abroad' but the effectiveness of the imperial application of such grants has been doubted. See Lionel Bently, 'The "Extraordinary Multiplicity" of Intellectual Property Laws in the British Colonies in the Nineteenth Century' (2011) 12(1) *Theoretical Inquiries in Law* 161, 163.

45. 'Patent Illuminating Map Printing', *South Australian* (Adelaide), 20 July 1841, 4.

46. 'New and Wonderful Discovery', *The Colonist* (Sydney), 11 December 1839, 4.

47. 'British Extracts: Lithography by Steam', *The Maitland Mercury and Hunter River General Advertiser* (Maitland), 23 August 1845, 4.

48. 'The Royal Society of Van Diemen's Land', *Launceston Examiner* (Launceston), 27 August 1851, 4.

49. 'Science, Art, and Manufacturers: Lithographic Printing Press', *Adelaide Observer* (Adelaide), 7 February 1846, 2.

50. In the colony of New South Wales see *Letters of Registration for Inventions Act 1852* (NSW). In the colony of Victoria see *Patent Act 1856* (Vic). In the colony of Tasmania see *Letters Patent for Inventions Act 1858* (Tas). In the colony of South Australia see *Patents Act 1859* (SA). In the colony of Queensland see *Provisional Registration of Inventions Act 1867* (Qld). As for the colony of Western Australia see *Grant of Patents Act 1872* (WA).

51. In fact, a search of the Victorian Gazettes for 'lithography' and 'printing' related patents during this period returned no results.

52. 'Lithographic Press', *The Australian* (Sydney), 24 October 1828, 4. Also see 'Classified Advertising', *Hobart Town Courier* (Hobart), 20 June 1829, 3.

53. Earl remained in Australia for three years, painting landscapes, studies of Aborigines and portraits of colonial notables, where he gained a reputation as the first professional artist to work in Australia. See Bernard Smith, *Earle, Augustus (1793-1838)* Australian Dictionary of Biography <http://adb.anu.edu.au/biography/earle-augustus-2016>.

54. Ibid.

55. Victorian Parliamentary Papers No. 11, 1860-61 (Melbourne, 1861).

56. Nicholas Chevalier, *Nicholas Chevalier's Album of Chromo Lithographs* (1865).

57. 'Lithographic Artists and Engravers' Club', *The Argus* (Melbourne), 22 February 1889, 4.

58. The works of S T Gill have been beautifully collated in Sasha Grishin, *S. T. Gill & His Audiences* (National Library of Australia Publishing with the State Library of Victoria, 2015).

59. See, eg, 'Latest British Extracts', *The Sydney Gazette and News South Wales Advertiser* (Sydney), 12 March 1828, 3 which reported on the use of compact limestone from Lisbon rather than the traditional source, Bavaria. Also see 'Knight's Illuminated Prints and Maps', *The Sydney Monitor and Commercial Advertiser* (Sydney), 18 March 1839, 7.

60. 'Domestic Intelligence', *The Monitor* (Sydney), 11 August 1826, 2. For more articles on the history of lithography and its invention by Alois Senefelder, see 'Lithography', *Snowy River Mail* (Orbost), 3 April 1913, 4.

61. Roger Butler, 'Lithography in Australia: Melbourne 1948-1958' in Pat Gilmour (ed), *Lasting Impressions: Lithographs as Art* (Australian National Gallery, 1988) 283, 283.

62. Joan Maslen, 'Theatre Posters of the Golden Age' (1981) 21 *The Australian Antique Collector* 65, 68.

63. 'The Calcutta Exhibition, Further Awards', *South Australian Register* (Adelaide), 20 February 1884, 5.

64. Harold Freedman, above n 24, 2.

65. See State Library Victoria, *Troedel Archive* <http://www.slv.vic.gov.au/search-discover/explore-collections-format/pictures/troedel-archive>.

Chapter II: In the Home

1. *Sydney Gazette and New South Wales Advertiser* (Sydney), 5 March 1803.

2. Juliann Sivulka, *Soap, Sex, and Cigarettes: A Cultural History of American Advertising* (Cengage Learning, 2nd ed, 2012) 64.

3. For a more expansive history of packaging or the 'pre-history' of packaging, see Alec Davis, *Package and Print: The Development of Container and Label Design* (Faber, 1967) 23-34.

4. Davis, above n 3.

5. Ibid 72.

6. See Diana Twede, 'The Birth of Modern Packaging: Cartons, Cans and Bottles' (2012) 4(2) *Journal of Historical Research in Marketing* 245, 245-72. Further see Diana Twede et al, *Cartons, Crates and Corrugated Board: Handbook of Paper and Wood Packaging Technology* (DEStech Publications Inc, 2nd ed, 2015) 1-70. Also see Harry J Bettendorf, *Paperboard and Paperboard Containers: A History* (Board Products Publishing, 1946).

7. Davis, above n 3, 25-32.

8. Ibid 26.

9. Ibid.

10. As cited in Marianne R Klimchuk and Sandra A Krasovec, *Packaging Design: Successful Product Branding from Concept to Shelf* (John Wiley & Sons, 2006) 13.

11. Ibid.

12. See generally A W Bitting, *Appertizing or The Art of Canning: Its History and Development* (Trade Pressroom, 1937). Also see Sara Risch, 'Food Packaging History and Innovations' (2009) 57(18) *Journal of Agricultural and Food Chemistry* 8089, 8089-92.

13. Susan Featherstone, 'A Review of Development in and Challenges of Thermal Processing over the Past 200 Years – A Tribute to Nicolas Appert' (2012) 47(2) *Food Research International* 156. See also Jane Busch, 'An Introduction to the Tin Can' (1981) 15(1) *Historical Archaeology* 95, 95-104.

14. Nicolas Appert, *The Art of Preserving All Kinds of Animal and Vegetable Substances for Several Years* (Black, Parry and Kingsbury, 1811).

15. Simon Naylor, 'Spacing the Can: Empire, Modernity, and the Globalisation of Food' (2000) 32 *Environment and Planning A* 1625.

16. Mary Ellen Snodgrass, *Encyclopedia of Kitchen History* (Fitzroy Dearborn, 2004) 162.

17. Davis, above n 3, 81.

18. E A Beaver, Elliott, Sizar (1814-1901) *Australian Dictionary of Biography* <http://adb.anu.edu.au/biography/elliott-sizar-3478>.

19. Tillie Stephens and Liza K Dale-Hallett, *Jam Factory – Factory & Companies Timeline* (2008) Museum Victoria Collections <http://collections.museumvictoria.com.au/articles/2686>.

20. 'Our Local Industries No. 5: W/D/ Peacock's Jam Factory', *The Tasmanian News* (Hobart), 5 August 1904, 3.

21. 'Messers. W.D. Peacock and Co's Jam Factory', *The Mercury* (Hobart), 7 March 1896, 3.

22. For example, the Brisbane publication *Truth* published a note on the brand which read: 'There are jams and jams, but none excels in quality and purity of component ingredients the famous brand "I.X.L.," which has been before the public for such a great number of years, and has acquired a wide popularity. Housewives who like something cheap, good, and tasty, should try it.' 'I.X.L Jam', *Truth* (Brisbane), 8 August 1909, 14.

23. 'Local Industries: Peacock's Jam Factory', *The Mercury Supplement* (Hobart), 12 February 1884, 1.

24. Ibid.

25. 'Industrial New South Wales: The Making of Jam, The Peacock's Company Factory', *The Australian Star* (Sydney), 2 February 1899, 3.

26. 'Messers. W.D. Peacock and Co's Jam Factory', above n 21, 3.

27. For more on the history of fonts and typeface see generally Phil Baines and Andrew Haslam, *Type and Typography* (Laurence King Publishing, 2nd ed, 2005).

28. Davis, above n 3, 92.

29. Ibid 92.

30. *1854 Australia's First Biscuit Company* Australian Food History Timeline <http://australianfoodtimeline.com.au/1854-australias-first-biscuit-company/>.

31. 'The Story of Our Secondary Industries', *The Age* (Melbourne), 23 January 1937, 7.

32. Philip E Muskett, *The Art of Living in Australia* (Sydney University Press, first published 1893, 2016 ed) 67.

33. See The University of Melbourne Archives, Robert Harper & Co Ltd (1896–1982) Accession Number 82/104, 89/110. For more on the life of Robert Harper, see Peter Cook, Harper, Robert (1842 – 1919) *Australian Dictionary of Biography* <http://adb.anu.edu.au/biography/harper-robert-6572>.

34. Ibid.

35. 'Robert Harper and Co's Australian Manufactures', *The Queenslander* (Brisbane), 19 June 1897, 1352.

36. Ibid.

37. Erika Rappaport, *A Thirst for Empire: How Tea Shaped the Modern World* (Princeton University Press, 2017). Also see Lizzie Collingham, *The Hungry Empire: How Britain's Quest for Food Shaped the Modern World* (Vintage Publishing, 2017).

38. In the United States, see Ross D Petty, 'From Label to Trademark: The Legal Origins of the Concept of Brand Identity in Nineteenth Century America' (2012) 4(1) *Journal of Historical Research in Marketing* 129, 129-53. In the United Kingdom, see Michael Jubb, *Cocoa and Corsets: A Selection of Late Victorian and Edwardian Posters and Showcards from the Stationers' Company Copyright Records Preserved in the Public Record Office* (Stationery Office Books, 1984).

39. *Scoville v Toland*, 21 F Cas 863, 864 (1848) (McClean J).

40. Ibid.

41. *George Bleistein v Donaldson Lithographing Company*, 188 US 239, 251 (1903).

42. J T Hood, *A Manual of the Law and Practice of Trade Mark Registration in Victoria* (Cuthbert & Co, 1892) Introduction.

43. In South Australia see *Trade Marks Act 1863* (SA). In Tasmania see *Merchandise Marks Act 1864* (Tas). In Queensland see *Trade Marks Act 1864* (Qld). In Victoria see *Trade Marks Statute 1864* (Vic) although this Act did not provide for trade mark registration. That came later in 1876. In New South Wales see *Trade Marks Act 1865* (NSW). In Western Australia see *Design and Trade Marks Act 1884* (WA). For more on the history of trade mark law in Australia see Amanda Scardamaglia, *Colonial Australian Trade Mark Law: Narratives in Lawmaking, People, Power and Place* (Australian Scholarly Publishing, 2015).

44. Amanda Scardamaglia, above n 43.

45. 'The Patents' Copyrights Office, Melbourne', *Evening News* (Sydney), 17 January 1879, 3.

46. Ibid.

47. Ibid.

48. *Leather Cloth Co v American Leather Cloth* (1865) 11 ER 1435 as cited in William Henry Browne, *A Treatise on the Law of Trade-Marks and Analogous Subjects* (Little, Brown, and Company, first published 1873, 1885 ed) §127.

49. See, eg, *Trade Marks Registration Act 1876* (Vic) s 2 where a trade mark was defined as including '[a] distinctive device mark heading label or ticket'.

50. The lack of case law was observed, both in Victoria and in the United Kingdom: 'The Patents' Copyrights Office, Melbourne', above n 45, 3.

51. Ibid.

52. For a critical examination of this case see Zvi S. Rosen, 'Reimagining Bleistein: Copyright for Advertisements in Historical Perspective' 59 (2012) *Journal of the Copyright Society in the USA* 347-389. Also see Barton Beebe, '"Bleistein", The Problem of Aesthetic Progress, and the Making of American Copyright Law (2017) 117(2) *Columbia Law Review* 319-397.

53. Starting with the seminal case of *A-G (NSW) ex rel Tooth & Co Ltd v Brewery Employees' Union of NSW* (1908) 6 CLR 469.

54. For more on the role of lithography in shaping the intellectual property system see generally Amanda Scardamaglia, 'A Legal History of Lithography' (2017) 26(1) *Griffith Law Review* 1-27. Also see Amanda Scardamaglia, 'Lithograph' in Claudy Op den Kamp and Dan Hunter (eds) *A History of IP in 50 Objects* (Oxford University Press, 2019).

Chapter III: At the Bar

1. Sherry Saggers and Dennis Gray, *Dealing with Alcohol: Indigenous Usage in Australia, New Zealand and Canada* (Cambridge University Press, 1998) 42-5.

2. Russel Ward, *The Australian Legend* (Oxford University Press, 1981) 35.

3. N G Butlin, 'Yo, Ho, Ho and How Many Bottles of Rum?' (1983) 23 *Australian Economic History Review* 1.

4. Ministerial Council on Drug Strategy, *Alcohol in Australia: Issues and Strategies* (July 2001) Australian Government Department of Health, <http://www.health.gov.au/internet/drugstrategy/publishing.nsf/Content/alc-strategy/%24FILE/alcohol_strategy_back.pdf>.

5. A G L Shaw, 'Some Aspects of New South Wales, 1788-1810' (1971) 57 *Journal of the Royal Australian Historical Society* 93-112.

6. *Humbug*, 15 September 1869.

7. Ibid.

8. David Collins, 'Collins's Account of the English Colony of New South Wales' in *Analytical Review: Or History of Literature, Domestic and Foreign, on an Enlarged Plan* (J Johnson, 1798) vol 28, 130.

9. Jack S Blocker, David M Fahey and Ian R Tyrrell (eds), *Alcohol and Temperance in Modern History: An International Encyclopaedia* (ABC-Clio, 2003) vol 1, 407-8.

10. Milton Lewis, *A Rum State: Alcohol and State Policy in Australia 1788-1988* (AGPS Press, 1992) 6.

11. On the use of alcohol for medicinal purposes see W S Campbell, 'The Use and Abuse of Stimulants in the Early Days of Settlement in New South Wales' (1932) 18 *Journal of Royal Australian Historical Society* 74, 77.

12. A E Dingle, '"The Truly Magnificent Thirst": An Historical Survey of Australian Drinking Habits' (1980) 19 *Historical Studies* 227, 229-30.

13. This is where the term the 'Rum State' comes from. See Lewis, above n 10.

14. *From Terra Australis to Australia* State Library New South Wales <http://www.sl.nsw.gov.au/stories/terra-australis-australia/1808-rum-rebellion>.

15. Grace Karskens and Richard Waterhouse, 'Too Sacred to Be Taken Away': Property, Liberty, Tyranny and the "Rum Rebellion"' (2010) 12 *Journal of Australian Colonial History* 1, 1-22.

16. For some alternative accounts of the rum rebellion see A G L Shaw, above n 5, 93-112. Also see Stephen Dando-Collins, *Captain Bligh's Other Mutiny: The True Story of the Military Coup that Turned Australia into a Two Year Rebel Republic* (Random House, 2007).

17. Jonathan King, *Great Moments in Australian History* (Allen & Unwin, 2009) 55.

18. Ross Fitzgerald, *Bligh, Macarthur and the Rum Rebellion* (Kangaroo Press, 1988).

19. Elizabeth Abbott, *Sugar: A Bittersweet History* (Duckworth Overlook, 2009) 134.

20. B W Higman, 'The Sugar Revolution' (2000) 53(2) *Economic History* 213, 213-36.

21. On this sad history see Abbott, above n 19.

22. Linda A Newson, 'The Demographic Collapse of Native Peoples of the Americas, 1492-1650' (1993) 81 *Proceedings of the British Academy* 247, 247-88.

23. Lizzie Collingham, *The Hungry Empire: How Britain's Quest for Food Shaped the Modern World* (Vintage Publishing, 2017).

24. Judith Iltis, Boston, John (?-1804) *Australian Dictionary of Biography* <http://adb.anu.edu.au/biography/boston-john-1804>.

25. David Dunstan, *Brewers and Brewing eMelbourne: The City Past & Present* <http://www.emelbourne.net.au/biogs/EM00232b.htm>.

26. Ibid.

27. Ibid.

28. George Parsons, de Bavay, Auguste Joseph François (1856–1944) *Australian Dictionary of Biography* <http://adb.anu.edu.au/biography/de-bavay-auguste-joseph-francois-5934>.

29. Ibid.

30. Ibid.

31. 'Typhoid Germs in Yan Yean Water', *The Argus* (Melbourne), 17 July 1889, 9.

32. 'Death of Mr A De Bavary: Scientist and Inventor', *The Argus* (Melbourne), 17 November 1944, 4.

33. Victorian Heritage Database Report, *Former Carlton & United Brewery* (Victorian Heritage Register Number H0024).

34. *Intellectual Property Development Company Pty Ltd v CUB Pty Ltd* [2013] ATMO 73 (10 September 2013) and *CUB Pty Ltd v Elixir Signature Pty Ltd* [2013] ATMO 74 (10 September 2013).

35. 'Lecture on Temperance', *The Colonist* (Sydney), 25 June 1835, 3.

36. 'Medical Testimonies', *The Teetotaller and General Newspaper* (Sydney), 5 March 1842, 4.

37. Ibid.

38. Ministerial Council on Drug Strategy, above n 4, 1.

39. Ian Tyrrell, 'The Anti-Tobacco Reform and the Temperance Movement in Australia: Connections and Differences' (1998) 84(1) *Journal of the Royal Australian Historical Society* 10, 10-25.

40. M Z Forbes, Bannerman, Charles (1851-1930) *Australian Dictionary of Biography* <http://adb.anu.edu.au/biography/bannerman-charles-2929>.

41. See, eg, Trade Mark Number 9167, *Victorian Trade Mark Register* (1905).

42. For a history of Melbourne's obsession with coffee, and coffee houses see Andrew Brown-May, *Espresso! Melbourne Coffee Stories* (Arcadia, 2001).

43. Elaine Denby, *Grand Hotels: Reality and Illusion* (Reaktion Books, 2002) 174.

44. For more see Max Allen, *The History of Australian Wine: Stories from the Vineyard to the Cellar Door* (Victory Books, 2012).

45. Philip E Muskett, *The Art of Living in Australia* (Sydney University Press, first published 1893, 2016 ed) 178.

46. *Penfolds History*, Penfolds <https://www.penfolds.com/en-au/about-penfolds/heritage/our-history>.

47. 'Mr H L Penfold Hyland, Wine Maker', Advocate (Burnie), 7 May 1940, 2.

48. *Burgoyne's Trade Mark* (1889) 6 RPC 227.

49. Ibid.

50. See Megan Richardson, Jill Klein and Julian Thomas, 'From 'Omoo' to 'Oro': Nostalgia Labels and Cultural Policy on the Australian Trade Marks Register' in Susy Frankel (ed) *The Object and Purpose of Intellectual Property* (Edward Elgar, forthcoming).

51. The term "barbarous language' was referenced in Duncan Kerly, *The Law of Trade Marks and Trade Names* (Stevens and Sons, 1894) 146.

52. Anne McClintock, 'Soft-Soaping Empire: Commodity Racism and Imperial Advertising' in N Mirzoeff (ed), *The Visual Cultural Reader* (Routledge, 1998), 304-5.

53. Richardson, above n 50.

Chapter IV: Health & Hygiene

1. 'Little's "Phenyle" Disinfectants', *The Argus* (Melbourne), 26 January 1899, 6.

2. 'Little's "Phenyle"', *Sydney Morning Herald* (Sydney), 28 April 1892, 6.

3. Museums Victoria, *Victorian Collections: Bottle: Phenyle* <https://victoriancollections.net.au/items/5191b1ae2162ef064c6ef6d7>.

4. Trade Mark Numbers 2391-2394, *Victorian Trade Mark Register* (1890).

5. Trade Mark Numbers 1064 and 1065, *Victorian Trade Mark Register* (1885).

6. 'Poisoning by Carbolic Acid', Australian *Town and Country Journal* (Sydney), 2 November 1872, 2.

7. Nicholas Mason, *Literary Advertising and the Shaping of British Romanticism* (John Hopkins University Press, 2013) 34.

8. Ibid.

9. 'Case under the Dental Act', *The Inquirer & Commercial News* (Perth), 28 June 1895, 4.

10. 'Mr Ralph Potts Dies', *The Daily News* (Perth), 14 March 1944, 3.

11. Potts was charged under sections 15(1) & (2) of the *Dentists Act 1894* (WA). Section 15(1) prohibited a person from using '... the name or title of "Dentist" or "Dental Surgeon," or any other name, words, title, or description, either alone or in conjunction with any other word or words implying or tending to the belief that he is entitled to practise dentistry or dental surgery ...' unless that person was registered as a dentist under the Act or as a medical practitioner under *The Medical Ordinance 1869* (WA). Section 15(2) prohibited a person from practising '... dentistry or dental surgery, or perform[ing] any dental operation or service ...' unless they were registered.

12. 'Case under the Dental Act', above n 9, 4.

13. 'The Dental Board and Mr. Ralph Potts', *The West Australian* (Perth), 25 October 1898, 7.

14. 'Case under the Dental Act', above n 9, 4.

15. 'Ralph Potts Again', *The Goldfields Morning Chronicle* (Coolgardie), 15 November 1897, 3.

16. 'The Dental Board and Mr. Ralph Potts', above n 13, 7.

17. 'Registration of Ralph Potts', *The Menzies Miner* (Western Australia), 24 September 1898, 20.

18. In Victoria for example see the *Dentists Act 1898* (Vic). In New South Wales see *Dentists Act 1900* (NSW).

19. On the history of the use of morphine as medicine see Barbara Hodgson, *In the Arms of Morpheus: The Tragic History of Laudanum, Morphine and Patent Medicines* (Greystone Books, 2008).

20. 'J Collis Browne's Chlorodyne' in Peter G Homan, Briony Hudson, and Raymond C Rowe, *Popular Medicines: An Illustrated History* (Pharmaceutical Press, 2007) 52-60.

21. 'For the Blood is the Life', *The Argus* (Melbourne), 24 July 1891, 4.

22. 'For the Blood is the Life: Clarke's Blood Mixture', *Geelong Advertiser* (Geelong), 2 June 1885, 3.

23. 'For the Blood is the Life: Clarke's Blood Mixture', *The McIvor Times and Rodney Advertiser* (Heathcote), 18 October 1900, 4.

24. British Medical Association, *Secret Remedies: What they Cost and What they Contain* (British Medical Association, 1908).

25. 'Clarke's Blood Mixture' in Peter G Homan, Briony Hudson, and Raymond C Rowe, *Popular Medicines: An Illustrated History* (Pharmaceutical Press, 2007) 49.

26. Labels for these products can be found in the Troedel archive. See *Moulton's Fruit Pills* (c 1880), State Library Victoria, Volume 10 and *Weston's Magic Pills* (c 1880), State Library Victoria, Volume 10.

27. 'Law Report: Eno v Davies and Another', *Sydney Morning Herald* (Sydney), 11 June 1884, 6.

28. 'Moulton's Blood Searcher', *Burra Record* (South Australia), 14 May 1879, 4.

29. See Edward Gilks (1822-?), *Elizabeth Street* (1864) (Charles Troedel, Melbourne Album Office, 1864), State Library Victoria, H600 and Edward Gilks (1822-?), *Flinders Street (From the Melbourne Railway Station)* (1864) (Charles Troedel, Melbourne Album Office, 1864), State Library Victoria, H3715.

30. 'Moulton's Pain Paint', *The McIvor Times and Rodney Advertiser* (Heathcote), 8 May 1879, 1.

31. 'Moulton's Pain Paint' (1884) 2(79) *The Bulletin* 21.

32. Ishmal, 'Various Verses. For the Bulletin. A Hymn to Humbug. Verses unto Vice. Quacks and their Victims.' (1884) 2(79) *The Bulletin* 22.

33. Ibid.

34. 'Moulton's Pain Paint', *Burra Record* (South Australia), 16 May 1879, 4.

35. 'Albany: From Our Correspondent', *Victorian Express* (Geraldton), 9 March 1861, 2.

36. 'Trade Mark Application Number 520' in Victoria, *Victoria Government Gazette*, No 19, 16 February 1877, 362.

37. Cedric Larson, 'Patent-Medicine Advertising and the Early American Press' (1937) 14(4) *Journalism and Mass Communication Quarterly* 333, 335.

38. *Sykes v Sykes* (1824) 3 B & C 541; 107 ER 834.

39. James Harvey Young, *The Toadstool Millionaires: A Social History of Patent Medicines in America before Federal Regulation* (Princeton University Press, 2nd ed, 1972). For a general history of patented medicines see Barbara Hodgson, above n 19, 103-24.

40. In Victoria for example see *Patent Act 1856* (Vic).

41. David Armstrong and Elizabeth Armstrong, *The Great American Medicine Show Being an Illustrated History of Hucksters, Healers, Health Evangelists, and Heroes from Plymouth Rock to the Present* (Prentice Hall, 1991) 160.

42. Commonwealth, Royal Commission on Secret Drugs, Cures and Foods, *Report* (1907) vol 1, 426.

43. John Mercer, *A Mark of Distinction: Branding and Trade Mark Law in the UK from the 1860s* (27 July 2009) SSRN <http://ssrn.com/abstract=1439750>.

44. Edward Hubbard and Michael Shippobottom, *A Guide to Port Sunlight Village: Including Two Tours of the Village* (Liverpool University Press, 2nd ed, 2005) 1.

45. For a general history of Port Sunlight see ibid.

46. Mercer, above n 43, 22.

47. The word SUNLIGHT was not registered as a trade mark in the United Kingdom until 1888, as word marks were not registrable before that time. For more on Sunlight soap and its branding see Amanda Scardamaglia, *Colonial Australian Trade Mark Law: Narratives in Lawmaking, People, Power and Place* (Australian Scholarly Publishing, 2015) 99-104.

48. David Eveleigh, *Bogs, Baths and Basins: The Story of Domestic Sanitation* (Sutton Publishing, 2002) 65.

49. Vincent Vinikas, *Soft Soap, Hard Sell: American Hygiene in an Age of Advertisement* (Iowa State University Press, 1992).

50. A E Musson, *Enterprise in Soap and Chemicals: Joseph Crosfield and Sons Ltd, 1815–1965* (Manchester University Press, 1965) 111.

51. Ibid.

52. Mercer, above n 43, 24-5.

53. Scardamaglia, above n 47, 36-47.

54. Juliann Sivulka, *Soap, Sex, and Cigarettes: A Cultural History of American Advertising* (Cengage Learning, 2nd ed, 2012) 64.

55. Edwin Barnard, *Emporium: Selling the Dream in Colonial Australia* (National Library of Australia Publishing, 2015) 97.

56. Thomas Brodribb, *Manual of Health and Temperance* (with Appendix on Infectious Diseases and Ambulance Work by John William Springthorpe) (Victorian Education Department, 1891).

57. Philip E Muskett, *The Art of Living in Australia* (Sydney University Press, first published 1893, 2016 ed) 25.

58. 'Lewis and Whitty's Exhibit', *Australian Town and Country Journal* (Sydney), 27 April 1895, 22.

59. 'Industries of the Colony XIII: Lewis and Whitty's Starch and Soap', *The Argus* (Melbourne), 20 June 1885, 5.

60. 'Death of Mr J.B. Whitty', *The Argus* (Melbourne), 2 December 1914, 8.

61. David Eveleigh, above n 48, 64.

62. Rudyard Kipling, 'The White Man's Burden', *The New York Sun* (New York), 10 February 1899.

63. Anne McClintock, *Imperial Leather: Race, Gender, and Sexuality in the Colonial Contest* (Routledge, 1995); Anandi Ramamurthy, Imperial Persuaders: Images of Africa and Asia in British Advertising (Manchester University Press, 2003) 34.

64. Michelle I Parker, *The Truth is in the Lye: Soap, Beauty, and Ethnicity in British Soap Advertisements* (History Undergraduate Thesis, Paper 7, University of Washington, 2014) <https://digitalcommons.tacoma.uw.edu/cgi/viewcontent.cgi?article=1008&context=history_theses>.

65. N K Fairbank Company Fairy Soap Advertisement, 'Why Doesn't Your Mamma Wash You with Fairy Soap' (c 1893) (Gray Lithograph Company, New York, 1893), Stanford Libraries, *American Broadsides and Ephemera*, First Series, 29523.

66. Pears' Soap Advertisement, 'The White Man's Burden' (1899), first published in *McClure's Magazine* (October 1899).

67. See, eg, Anne McClintock, above n 63; Anandi Ramamurthy, above n 63; Michelle I Parker, above n 64.

68. Pears' Soap Advertisement, 'Pears Transparent Soap' (1884).

Chapter V: Fashion & Style

1. Juliann Sivulka, *Soap, Sex, and Cigarettes: A Cultural History of American Advertising* (Cengage Learning, 2nd ed, 2012) 44.

2. Ibid.

3. 'To the Printer of the Sydney Gazette', *Sydney Gazette & New South Wales Advertiser* (Sydney), 12 November 1890, 2.

4. Sivulka, above n 1, 44.

5. For more see 'Families, Relationships and Home Life', in Kathryn Gleadle, *British Women in the Nineteenth Century* (Palgrave, 2001) 37.

6. 'Sewing Machines' in Mary Ellen Snodgrass, *World Clothing and Fashion: An Encyclopedia of History, Culture, and Social Influence* (Routledge, 2015) 507, 507-9. Also see Ruth Brandon, *A Capitalist Romance: Singer and the Sewing Machine* (Lippincott, 1979).

7. United States Patent Number 8294 (12 August 1851).

8. *The World of Fashion and Continental Feuilletons* (London, 1824-1851). In 1852, this merged with *The Ladies' Monthly Magazine* and became known as *Ladies Monthly Magazine, the World of Fashion, Journal of Fashion, Literature, Music, the Opera, and the Theatres*.

9. *Ladies Monthly Magazine, the World of Fashion, Journal of Fashion, Literature, Music, the Opera, and the Theatres* (Simpkin, Marshall & Co, 1852-1879).

10. Cristina Giorcelli, 'Introduction: Fashioning a Century' in Cristina Giorcelli and Paula Rabinowitz (eds) *Fashioning the Nineteenth Century: Habits of Being* (University of Minnesota Press, 2014) 3-4.

11. Alison Gernsheim, *Victorian and Edwardian Fashion: A Photographic Survey* (Dover Publications, 1982) 45.

12. British Patent Number 1729 (22 July 1856).

13. Gernsheim, above n 11, 46.

14. *Crinoline und Amazonenhut* (Nordhausen, 2nd ed, 1858).

15. 'Crinolineomania: Treated Pathologically by Dr. Punch', Punch (London), 27 December 1856, 253.

16. Karen Bowman, Corsets and Codpieces: *A History of Outrageous Fashion, From Roman Times to the Modern Era* (Pen & Sword Books, 2015) 92-93.

17. Ibid.

18. Emily Westkaemper, *Selling Women's History: Packaging Feminism in Twentieth-Century American Popular Culture* (Rutgers University Press, 2017) 1.

19. 'Robertson & Moffat', *Illustrated Australian News* (Melbourne), 3 October 1878, 176.

20. Robertson & Moffat Pty Ltd, *Wedding Gown* (Melbourne, 1892) National Gallery Victoria Accession Number D101-1971.

21. 'Messrs, Craig, Williamson, & Thomas's Establishment', *Frearson's Monthly Illustrated Adelaide News* (Adelaide), 1 March 1881, 35.

22. James Lever, *Fashions and Fashion Plates 1800-1900* (Penguin Books, 1943) 3.

23. 'Corset Department', *Sydney Mail & New South Wales Advertiser* (Sydney), 20 October 1894, 808.

24. Tom Reichert, *The Erotic History of Advertising* (Prometheus Books, 2003).

25. Jim Aitchison, *Cutting Edge Advertising* (Prentice Hall, 1999) 8.

26. Bob Garfield, *And Now A Few Words From Me* (McGraw Hill, 2003) 63.

27. Jean Boddewyn, 'Controlling Sex and Decency in Advertising Around the World' (1991) 20(4) *Journal of Advertising* 25, 25.

28. Ibid.

29. As advertised in *London Evening Standard* (London), 15 August 1862, 1. For more on the rise and fall of the 1862 invention see Rebecca Mitchell, '15 August 1862: The Rise and Fall of the Cage Crinoline' (2016) *University of Birmingham Research Portal* <https://research.birmingham.ac.uk/portal/files/29075836/Mitchell_Crinoline_Pre_Print.pdf>.

30. US Patent Number US33517A (22 October 1861). This patent was awarded to Henry Cook for 'Improvements in Hoop-Skirts'.

31. B Zorina Khan, '"Not for Ornament": Patenting Activity by Nineteenth-Century Women Inventors' (2000) 33(2) *Journal of Interdisciplinary History* 159, 159-95.

32. Kara W Swanson, 'Corset' in Claudy Op den Kamp and Dan Hunter (eds) *A History of IP in 50 Objects* (Oxford University Press, 2019).

33. Ibid.

34. Kara W Swanson, 'Getting a Grip on the Corset: Gender, Sexuality and Patent Law' (2011) 23 Y*ale Law Journal & Feminism* 57, 57-115.

35. 'The Corset Case', *Sunday Times* (Perth), 14 January 1906, 3.

36. Ibid.

37. 'The Great Corset Case', *The Sydney Morning Herald* (Sydney), 20 April 1905, 9.

38. *Re Weingarten Brothers' Trade Mark* (1904) 29 VLR 965.

39. *Re Weingarten Brothers* (1903) 9 ALR 268a.

40. *Re Weingarten Brothers' Trade Mark* (1904) 29 VLR 965, 977 (Madden CJ).

41. 'The Corset Case', above n 35, 3.

42. Ibid.

43. 'The Celebrated Corset Case', *Ovens and Murray Advertiser* (Beechworth), 30 December 1905, 1.

44. 'The Corset Case', *Observer* (Adelaide), 16 June 1906, 43.

45. *Weingarten Brothers v G & R Wills & Co* [1906] SALR 34.

46. J J Bray, *Way, Sir Samuel James (1836-1916) Australian Dictionary of Biography* <http://adb.anu.edu.au/biography/way-sir-samuel-james-9014>.

47. Albert James Hannan, *The Life of Chief Justice Way: A Biography of the Right Honourable Sir Samuel Way* (Angus and Robertson, 1960).

48. John Hood, *Australia and the East* (Murray, 1843) 89.

49. 'Ladies' Column: The Sewing Machine', *The Illustrated Sydney News and New South Wales Agriculturalist and Grazier* (Sydney), 26 October 1872, 4.

50. *The Argus* (Melbourne), 12 April 1877, 4.

51. Ibid.

52. Ibid.

53. 'Fashions for September: From Le Follet', *The Argus*, (Melbourne), 28 November 1861, 3.

54. 'Fashion for August', *The Argus* (Melbourne), 25 September 1861, 5.

55. 'Fashion by Harry Furniss in "St James's Budget"', *The Argus* (Melbourne), 20 May 1893, 13.

56. 'Clothes for Queensland', *Queensland Figaro* (Brisbane), 11 February 1888, 10.

57. Philip E Muskett, *The Art of Living in Australia* (Sydney University Press, first published 1893, 2016 ed) 46.

Chapter VI: Leisurely Pursuits

1. A E P Duffy, 'The Eight Hours Day Movement in Britain, 1886-1893' (1968) 36(3) *The Manchester School* 203, 203-22.

2. Victorian Operative Masons' Society, *Report of the Committee appointed by the Victorian Operative Masons' Society to inquire into the origin of the Eight-Hours' Movement in Victoria* (Walker May Printers, 1884) <http://ergo.slv.vic.gov.au/explore-history/fight-rights/workers-rights/origins-8-hour-day> (adopted at the annual meeting on 11 June 1884).

3. For more see Julie Kimber and Peter Love (eds), *The Time of Their Lives: The Eight Hour Day and Working Life* (Australian Society for the Study of Labour History, 2007). Also see Peter Love, 'Melbourne Celebrates the 150th Anniversary of its Eight Hour Day' [2006] (91) *Labour History* 193, 193-6.

4. Deborah Tout-Smith, James Galloway, *Leader of the Eight Hour Day Movement (1828-1860)* Museums Victoria <https://collections.museumvictoria.com.au/articles/2099>.

5. *The British Trade Journal & Export World*, vol 20 (1 March 1882) 162.

6. Ibid.

7. 'Bicycling', *Weekly Times* (Melbourne), 14 February 1885, 6.

8. 'New Premises for the Melbourne Sports Depot', *Prahran Chronicle* (Melbourne), 3 May 1902, 3.

9. Victoria Heritage Database Report, *Former Melbourne Sports Depot* (Hermes Number 64829).

10. 'Foy & Gibson', *The Argus* (Melbourne), 13 May 1872, 3.

11. 'Foy & Gibson's Annual Toy Fair and Magic Cave', *The Herald* (Melbourne), 13 December 1893, 1.

12. Collingwood Historical Society Inc, *Former Foy & Gibson Factory Buildings* <http://collingwoodhs.org.au/resources/collingwood-history-plaques-project/former-foy-gibson-factory-buildings/>.

13. Annette Shiell, *Fundraising, Flirtation and Fancywork: Charity Bazaars in Nineteenth Century Australia* (Cambridge Scholars Publishing, 2012) 2.

14. Ibid 6.

15. F K Prochaska, *Women and Philanthropy in Nineteenth-Century England* (Clarendon Press, 1980).

16. Shiell, above n 13, 8.

17. Ibid 8.

18. Ibid.

19. 'Melbourne Tea-Table Talk', *The West Australian* (Perth), 13 December 1886, 3.

20. Ibid.

21. Shiell, above n 13, 230.

22. 'The Contributor: Notes Now and Then', *The Australasian* (Melbourne), 11 August 1883, 3.

23. Joan Maslen, 'Theatre Posters of the Golden Age' [1981] (21) *Australian Antique Collector* 65, 69.

24. Ibid 67.

25. Sarah Suzuki, 'Toulouse-Lautrec: Life and Lithography', in *The Paris of Toulouse-Lautrec Prints and Posters from the Museum of Modern Art* (Museum of Modern Art, 2014) 9, 9.

26. The term is in reference to *Le Peintre Graveur*, a 21 volume catalogue of old master prints published by Johann Adam Bernhard Ritter von Bartsch between 1803 and 1821.

27. Suzuki, above n 25, 13.

28. Edmond de Goncourt, Journal (19 April 1884) 334.

29. Amanda Dunsmore, Matthew Martin and Wayne Crothers, *Japonisme: Japan and the Birth of Modern Art* (National Gallery of Victoria, 2018).

30. Olga Tsara, 'Troedel & Co: Master Printers and Lithographers,' [1998] (62) *La Trobe Journal* 30, 36.

31. Clive Turnbull (ed), 'The Melbourne Album': *Comprising a Series of Elegant, Tinted, Lithographic Views of Melbourne and Surrounding Districts Lithographed, Printed and Published by Charles Troedel in 1863* (Georgian House, 1961) 17.

32. Ibid 17.

33. Maslen, above n 23, 67.

34. Joan Maslen, 'The Golden Age of Melbourne Theatre' (1995) 66(2) *Victorian Historical Journal* 137, 137.

35. 'Tragedy at the Opera House', *The Brisbane Courier* (Brisbane), 2 August 1880, 3.

36. Ibid.

37. 'The Opera-House Disaster', *Weekly Times* (Melbourne) 20 September 1884, 12.

38. Mimi Colligan and Elisabeth Kumm, *Opera House* eMelbourne: The City Past & Present <http://www.emelbourne.net.au/biogs/EM01092b.htm>.

39. 'The Colonel', *The Argus* (Melbourne), 10 April 1882, 6.

40. Ibid.

41. 'Opera House', *The Argus* (Melbourne), 14 May 1883, 8.

42. Turnbull, above n 31, 19.

43. Elly Fink, *Young, William Blamire (1862–1935)* Australian Dictionary of Biography <http://adb.anu.edu.au/biography/young-william-blamire-9218>.

44. Bernard Smith, *Place, Taste and Tradition: A Study of Australian Art Since 1788* (Oxford University Press, 2nd revised ed, 1979).

45. David Raizman, *History of Modern Design* (Laurence King Publishing, 2003) 42.

46. John Ruskin, *The Elements of Drawing* (George Allen, 1898) 347.

47. Clinton Adams, 'The Nature of Lithography' in Pat Gilmour (ed) *Lasting Impressions: Lithographs as Art* (University of Pennsylvania Books, 1988) 29-32.

48. Ibid 33.

49. Pat Gilmour, 'Lithographic Collaboration: The Hand, the Head, the Heart' in Pat Gilmour (ed) *Lasting Impressions: Lithographs as Art* (University of Pennsylvania Books, 1988) 308. Further see Raymond Williams, *Keywords: A Vocabulary of Culture and Society* (Oxford University Press, 1976) 179.

50. Gilmour, above n 49, 308.

51. Ibid.

52. Alois Senefelder, *A Complete Course on Lithography* (A S trans, Ackermann, 1819) 179.

53. Raucourt de Charleville, *A Manual of Lithography* (Rodwell and Martin, 1820) 93-4.

54. 'Alexandra Theatre: Opening Night', *The Argus* (Melbourne), 2 October 1886, 10.

55. Ibid.

56. Martha Rutledge, *Joubert, Jules François de Sales (1824–1907)* Australian Dictionary of Biography <http://adb.anu.edu.au/biography/joubert-jules-francois-de-sales-3874>.

57. 'The Criterion Theatre', *Sydney Mail and New South Wales Advertiser* (Sydney), 12 May 1888, 1006.

58. 'The Criterion Theatre', *Sydney Morning Herald* (Sydney), 7 May 1888, 8.

59. Ibid.

Conclusion

1. Peter C Marzio, 'Lithography as a Democratic Art: A Reappraisal' (1971) 4(1) *Leonardo* 37-48.

2. Edwin L Godkin 'Chromo-Civilization' 19(482) (24 September 1874) *The Nation* 201-202.

3. Louis Prang, 'Art Critics Criticised' in *Prang's Chromo 1: A Journal of Popular Art* (L Prang and Company, 1868)

4. Walter Benjamin, 'The Work of Art in the Age of Mechanical Reproduction', in Hannah Arendt (ed) *Illuminations* (Harry Zohn trans, Schocken Books, 1968).

5. Above n 2.

6. Robert J Chandler, *San Francisco Lithographer: African American Artist Grafton Tyler Brown* (University of Oklahoma Press, 2014) 4.

7. On the concept of 'wild art' see David Carrier and Joachim Pissarro, *Wild Art* (Phaidon, 2013).

8. In Australia, see Sasha Grishin, *S. T. Gill & His Audiences* (National Library of Australia Publishing with the State Library of Victoria, 2015). Also see Edwin Barnard, *Emporium: Selling the Dream in Colonial Australia* (National Library of Australia Publishing, 2015) which includes a collection of historical advertising lithographs.

List of Illustrations

All illustrations are part of the Troedel Archive held at State Library Victoria, unless otherwise stated.

Cover

Robert Harper & Co's Assorted Labels (c 1880)
State Library Victoria, Miscellaneous

Inside Front Cover

Extract from *Winter, 1886* (c 1886)
State Library Victoria, Volume 20

Introductory Pages

The Reigning Cigarette, "Cameo" (1881-1900)
State Library Victoria, H2000.180/266

Mr Charles Troedel (1968)
State Library Victoria, H31630

Briar L.B.M. Pipes (c 1881-1890)
State Library Victoria, H2008.91/27

Silver Star Starch. One People, One Starch (c 1891-1900)
State Library Victoria, H2000.180/50

Victory Bitters (c 1872)
State Library Victoria, H96.160/2131

'Standard' Cushion Head Lining (c 1880-1890)
State Library Victoria, H2000.180/223

Introduction

Mr Frank Thornton's 5th Australasian Tour. On a Wave of Laughter (c 1890-1895)
State Library Victoria, H2000.180/45

Illustration of Charles Troedel's Occupation and Address (1870)
State Library Victoria, H96.160/1387

Awarded First Prize, Melbourne International Exhibition (1881)
State Library Victoria, H96.160/2078

Chapter I: The Visual Century

The Australasian Illustrated Weekly (c 1881-1890)
State Library Victoria, H2000.212/11

Photographer unknown, *Johannes Theodore Carl (Charles) Troedel and Julia Sarah Troedel (nee Glover and their family)* (c 1895)
Troedel Family Archive

Photographer unknown, *Employees of Charles Troedel & Co March 1899* (1889)
State Library Victoria, H2011.190a

Photographer unknown, *Employees of Charles Troedel & Co March 1899* (1889)
State Library Victoria, H2011.190b

Photographer unknown, *Employees of Charles Troedel & Co March 1899* (1889)
State Library Victoria, H2011.190c

Richard Wendel (1851-1926), *Middle Harbour, Sydney, New South Wales* (1878)
Published by Troedel & Co, Lithographers, Sydney
State Library Victoria, 30328102131777/7

Richard Wendel (1851-1926), *Botanical Gardens (Farm Cover) Government House in Distance* (1878)
Published by Troedel & Co, Lithographers, Sydney
State Library Victoria, 30328102131777/3

Charles Troedel Lithographer (c 1870)
Troedel Family Archive

Chapter II: In the Home

R.H. & Co. New Season's Teas For Sale Here. Brisbane 1890-1891 (1890)
State Library Victoria, H2000.180/114

Yorick Bacon and Hams (c 1881-1890)
State Library Victoria, H2008.94/46

I Come Full Speed to Tell You Peacock's Jams & Jellies Cannot be Excelled (c 1881-1890)
State Library Victoria, H2008.94/20

Robert Harper & Co's Assorted Labels (c 1880)
State Library Victoria, Miscellaneous

One Pound Canister Coffee (1871)
State Library Victoria, Accession Number H96.160/2100

Richard Wendel (1851-1926), *T. B. Guest & Co. Steam Biscuit Factory, William Street Melbourne* (1878)
State Library Victoria, H2000.180/195

T. B. Guest & Co. Steam Biscuit Factory, William Street Melbourne (c 1870-1879)
State Library Victoria, H2000.180/200

The Tea of the Times (1888)
State Library Victoria, H2000.180/109

The Hindoo Blend Pure Tea (c 1880-1890)
State Library Victoria, H2000.180/110

New Season's Teas 1891-1892 (c 1891)
State Library Victoria, Miscellaneous

Charles Turner (active 1869-1900), *The Oriental Tea Company Packet Tea* (c 1881-1890)
State Library Victoria, H2000.212/10

Licensed Victuallers Two Star Tea Association (1876)
State Library Victoria, H96.160/2408

Superior Raspberry Vinegar (1872)
State Library Victoria, H96.160/2136

Chapter III: At the Bar

The Celebrated Red Tag Tobacco Camerons (c 1881-1890)
State Library Victoria, H2008.94/90

Three Men Drinking and Smoking (c 1880-1900)
State Library Victoria, H2000.180/151

The Prince of Wales Finest Old Scotch Blend Whisky (c 1881-1890)
State Library Victoria, H2008.94/81

Finest Standard Old Vintage Brandy Cognac (c 1871)
State Library Victoria, H96.160/2124

Superior Jamaica Rum (c 1851-1885)
State Library Victoria, H32088/12

Finest Jamaica Rum (c 1875)
State Library Victoria, H96.160/2274

Old Jamaica Rum (c 1875)
State Library Victoria, H96.160/2436

Elliott's XXX Stout & Ales on Draught (c 1880-1890)
State Library Victoria, H2000.180/178

Carlton Prize Ale, Edward Latham (c 1875-1883)
State Library Victoria, H2000.180/255

Richard Wendel (1851-1926), *Carlton Brewery: The Melbourne Brewing & Malting Company Limited* (c 1875)
State Library Victoria, H2000.212/3

Try the Australian Trent Brewery's Pure Malt & Hop Ales (c 1881-1900)
State Library Victoria, H2000.180/248

Castlemaine Standard Brewing Coy's Fine Ales (c 1881-1900)
State Library Victoria, H2000.180/193

Bull Dog Brand R. Porter & Co. London (c 1881-1900)
State Library Victoria, H2000.180/210

Nordhausen Lager Beer. Schreiber & Schaefer. Little Flinders Street, West Melbourne. Sole Agents for Australia (c 1881-1900)
State Library Victoria, H2000.180/203

Smoke Smoke Cigarettes 3D Packet (c 1881-1890)
State Library Victoria, H2000.180/221

T.C. Williams & Co. Mabel Cut Plug (c 1881-1890)
State Library Victoria, H2008.94/48

The Cricketer (c 1880)
State Library Victoria, Volume 11

The Champion Virginian Tobacco (c 1881-1900)
State Library Victoria, H2000.180/240

Australian Moet Non-Alcoholic, Prepared by Geo. H. Bennett, Richmond (c 1881-1890)
State Library Victoria, H2008.94/88

Bibliography

Articles/Books/Reports

Abbott, Elizabeth, *Sugar: A Bittersweet History* (Duckworth Overlook, 2009)

Adams, Clinton, 'The Nature of Lithography' in Pat Gilmour (ed), *Lasting Impressions: Lithographs as Art* (Australian National Gallery, 1988) 25

Aitchison, Jim, *Cutting Edge Advertising* (Prentice Hall, 1999)

'Albany: From Our Correspondent', *Victorian Express* (Geraldton), 9 March 1861, 2

'Alexandra Theatre: Opening Night', *The Argus* (Melbourne), 2 October 1886, 10

Allen, Max, *The History of Australian Wine: Stories from the Vineyard to the Cellar Door* (Victory Books, 2012)

Appert, Nicolas, *The Art of Preserving All Kinds of Animal and Vegetable Substances for Several Years* (Black, Parry and Kingsbury, 1811)

Armstrong, David and Elizabeth Armstrong, *The Great American Medicine Show Being an Illustrated History of Hucksters, Healers, Health Evangelists, and Heroes from Plymouth Rock to the Present* (Prentice Hall, 1991)

Baines, Phil and Andrew Haslam, *Type and Typography* (Laurence King Publishing, 2nd ed, 2005)

Barnard, Edwin, *Emporium: Selling the Dream in Colonial Australia* (National Library of Australia Publishing, 2015)

Barthes, Roland, *Writing Degree Zero and Elements of Semiology* (A Lavers & C Smith trans, Beacon, 1970)

Beebe, Barton, '"Bleistein", The Problem of Aesthetic Progress, and the Making of American Copyright Law' (2017) 117(2) *Columbia Law Review* 319

Bently, Lionel, 'The "Extraordinary Multiplicity" of Intellectual Property Laws in the British Colonies in the Nineteenth Century' (2011) 12(1) *Theoretical Inquiries in Law* 161

Bettendorf, Harry J, *Paperboard and Paperboard Containers: A History* (Board Products Publishing, 1946)

'Bicycling', *Weekly Times* (Melbourne), 14 February 1885, 6

Bitting, A W, *Appertizing or The Art of Canning: Its History and Development* (Trade Pressroom, 1937)

Blocker, Jack S, David M Fahey and Ian R Tyrrell (eds), *Alcohol and Temperance in Modern History: An International Encyclopaedia* (ABC-Clio, 2003) vol 1

Boddewyn, Jean, 'Controlling Sex and Decency in Advertising Around the World' (1991) 20(4) *Journal of Advertising* 25

Bowman, Karen, *Corsets and Codpieces: A History of Outrageous Fashion, From Roman Times to the Modern Era* (Pen & Sword Books, 2015)

Brandon, Ruth, *A Capitalist Romance: Singer and the Sewing Machine* (Lippincott, 1979)

Brown-May, Andrew, *Espresso! Melbourne Coffee Stories* (Arcadia, 2001)

Benjamin, Walter, 'The Work of Art in the Age of Mechanical Reproduction', in Hannah Arendt (ed) *Illuminations* (Harry Zohn trans, Schocken Books, 1968)

Berelson, Bernard, *Content Analysis in Communication Research* (The Free Press, 1952)

'British Extracts: Lithography by Steam', *The Maitland Mercury and Hunter River General Advertiser* (Maitland), 23 August 1845, 4

British Medical Association, *Secret Remedies: What they Cost and What they Contain* (British Medical Association, 1908)

Brodribb, Thomas, *Manual of Health and Temperance (with Appendix on Infectious Diseases and Ambulance Work by John William Springthorpe)* (Victorian Education Department, 1891)

Bryans, Dennis, *A Seed of Consequence: Indirect Image Transfer and Chemical Printing: The Role Played by Lithography in the Development of Printing Technology* (PhD Thesis, Swinburne University of Technology, 2000)

Budd, R W, R K Thorp, and L Donohew, *Content Analysis of Communications* (Macmillan, 1967)

Busch, Jane, 'An Introduction to the Tin Can' (1981) 15(1) *Historical Archaeology* 95

Butlin, N G, 'Yo, Ho, Ho and How Many Bottles of Rum?' (1983) 23 *Australian Economic History Review* 1

Campbell, W S, 'The Use and Abuse of Stimulants in the Early Days of Settlement in New South Wales' (1932) 18 *Journal of Royal Australian Historical Society* 74

Carrier, David, and Pissarro, Joachim, *Wild Art* (Phaidon, 2013)

'Case under the Dental Act', *The Inquirer & Commercial News* (Perth), 28 June 1895, 4

Chandler, Robert J, *San Francisco Lithographer: African American Artist Grafton Tyler Brown* (University of Oklahoma Press, 2014)

Chevalier, Nicholas, *Nicholas Chevalier's Album of Chromo Lithographs* (1865)

'City Fire: Troedel's Printing Works Gutted', *The Australasia* (Melbourne), 13 February 1904, 29

'Classified Advertising', *Hobart Town Courier* (Hobart), 20 June 1829, 3

'Clothes for Queensland', *Queensland Figaro* (Brisbane), 11 February 1888, 10

Collingham, Lizzie, *The Hungry Empire: How Britain's Quest for Food Shaped the Modern World* (Vintage Publishing, 2017)

Collins, David, 'Collins's Account of the English Colony of New South Wales' in *Analytical Review: Or History of Literature, Domestic and Foreign, on an Enlarged Plan* (J Johnson, 1798) vol 28

Commonwealth, Royal Commission on Secret Drugs, Cures and Foods, *Report* (1907) vol 1

'Corset Department', *Sydney Mail & New South Wales Advertiser* (Sydney), 20 October 1894, 808

Crary, Jonathan, *Techniques of the Observer* (MIT Press, 1990)

'Crinolineomania: Treated Pathologically by Dr. Punch', *Punch* (London), 27 December 1856, 253

Crinoline und Amazonenhut (Nordhausen, 2nd ed, 1858)

Dando-Collins, Stephen, *Captain Bligh's Other Mutiny: The True Story of the Military Coup that Turned Australia into a Two Year Rebel Republic* (Random House, 2007)

Davis, Alec, *Package and Print: The Development of Container and Label Design* (Faber, 1967)

'Death of Mr A De Bavary: Scientist and Inventor', *The Argus* (Melbourne), 17 November 1944, 4

'Death of Mr J.B. Whitty', *The Argus* (Melbourne), 2 December 1914, 8

de Charleville, Raucourt, *A Manual of Lithography* (Rodwell and Martin, 1820)

de Goncourt, Edmond, *Journal* (19 April 1884)

Denby, Elaine, *Grand Hotels: Reality and Illusion* (Reaktion Books, 2002)

de Saussure, Ferdinand, *A Course in General Linguistics* (W Baskin trans, McGraw-Hill, 1966)

Dingle, A E, '"The Truly Magnificent Thirst": An Historical Survey of Australian Drinking Habits' (1980) 19 *Historical Studies* 227

Duffy, A E P, 'The Eight Hours Day Movement in Britain, 1886-1893' (1968) 36(3) *The Manchester School* 203

Dunsmore, Amanda, Matthew Martin and Crothers, Wayne, *Japonisme: Japan and the Birth of Modern Art* (National Gallery of Victoria, 2018)

Eco, Umberto, *A Theory of Semiotics* (Indiana University Press, 1976)

Engelmann, Godefroy, *Manuel du Dessinateur Lithographe* (Chez l'auteur, 1822)

Eveleigh, David, *Bogs, Baths and Basins: The Story of Domestic Sanitation* (Sutton Publishing, 2002)

Exposé, *The Argus* (Melbourne), 12 April 1877, 4

'Fashion by Harry Furniss in "St James's Budget"', *The Argus* (Melbourne), 20 May 1893, 13

'Fashion for August', *The Argus* (Melbourne), 25 September 1861, 5

'Fashions for September: From Le Follet', *The Argus*, (Melbourne), 28 November 1861, 3

Featherstone, Susan, 'A Review of Development in and Challenges of Thermal Processing over the Past 200 Years – A Tribute to Nicolas Appert' (2012) 47(2) *Food Research International* 156

Fitzgerald, Ross, *Bligh, Macarthur and the Rum Rebellion* (Kangaroo Press, 1988)

'For the Blood is the Life', *The Argus* (Melbourne), 24 July 1891, 4

'For the Blood is the Life: Clarke's Blood Mixture', *Geelong Advertiser* (Geelong), 2 June 1885, 3

'For the Blood is the Life: Clarke's Blood Mixture', *The McIvor Times and Rodney Advertiser* (Heathcote), 18 October 1900, 4

'Foy and Gibson', *The Argus* (Melbourne), 13 May 1872, 3

'Foy & Gibson's Annual Toy Fair and Magic Cave', *The Herald* (Melbourne), 13 December 1893, 1

Freedman, Harold, *The Book of Melbourne and Canberra: A Collection of Six Lithograph Prints of Melbourne Drawn in 1962-1963* (Griffin Press, 1966)

Garfield, Bob, *And Now A Few Words From Me* (McGraw Hill, 2003)

'German Emigration', *Port Phillip Gazette & Settler's Journal* (Melbourne), 9 December 1846, 2

Gernsheim, Alison, *Victorian and Edwardian Fashion: A Photographic Survey* (Dover Publications, 1982)

Giorcelli, Cristina, 'Introduction: Fashioning a Century' in Cristina Giorcelli and Paula Rabinowitz (eds) *Fashioning the Nineteenth Century: Habits of Being* (University of Minnesota Press, 2014)

Gilmour, Pat, 'Lithographic Collaboration: The Hand, the Head, the Heart' in Pat Gilmour (ed) *Lasting Impressions: Lithographs as Art* (University of Pennsylvania Books, 1988)

Gleadle, Kathryn, *British Women in the Nineteenth Century* (Palgrave, 2001)

Godkin, Edwin L, 'Chromo-Civilization' 19(482) (24 September 1874) *The Nation* 201

Grishin, Sasha, *S. T. Gill & His Audiences* (National Library of Australia Publishing with the State Library of Victoria, 2015)

Hannan, Albert James, *The Life of Chief Justice Way: A Biography of the Right Honourable Sir Samuel Way* (Angus and Robertson, 1960)

Higman, B W, 'The Sugar Revolution' (2000) 53(2) *Economic History* 213

Hodgson, Barbara, *In the Arms of Morpheus: The Tragic History of Laudanum, Morphine and Patent Medicines* (Greystone Books, 2008)

Homan, Peter G, Briony Hudson, and Raymond C Rowe, *Popular Medicines: An Illustrated History* (Pharmaceutical Press, 2007)

Hood, John, *Australia and the East* (Murray, 1843)

Hood, J T, *A Manual of the Law and Practice of Trade Mark Registration in Victoria* (Cuthbert & Co, 1892)

Hubbard, Edward and Michael Shippobottom, *A Guide to Port Sunlight Village: Including Two Tours of the Village* (Liverpool University Press, 2nd ed, 2005)

'Industrial New South Wales: The Making of Jam, The Peacock's Company Factory', *The Australian Star* (Sydney), 2 February 1899, 3

'Industries of the Colony XIII: Lewis and Whitty's Starch and Soap', *The Argus* (Melbourne), 20 June 1885, 5

Ishmal, 'Various Verses. For the Bulletin. A Hymn to Humbug. Verses unto Vice. Quacks and their Victims.' (1884) 2(79) *The Bulletin* 22

'I.X.L Jam', *Truth* (Brisbane), 8 August 1909, 14

Jensz, Felicity, *German Moravian Missionaries in the British Colony of Victoria, Australia, 1848-1908: Influential Strangers* (Brill, 2010)

Jubb, Michael, *Cocoa and Corsets: A Selection of Late Victorian and Edwardian Posters and Showcards from the Stationers' Company Copyright Records Presented in the Public Record Office* (Stationery Office Books, 1984)

Karskens, Grace and Richard Waterhouse, 'Too Sacred to Be Taken Away': Property, Liberty, Tyranny and the "Rum Rebellion"' (2010) 12 *Journal of Australian Colonial History* 1

Kerly, Duncan, *The Law of Trade Marks and Trade Names* (Stevens and Sons, 1894)

Khan, B Zorina, '"Not for Ornament": Patenting Activity by Nineteenth-Century Women Inventors' (2000) 33(2) *Journal of Interdisciplinary History* 159

Kimber, Julie and Peter Love (eds), *The Time of Their Lives: The Eight Hour Day and Working Life* (Australian Society for the Study of Labour History, 2007)

King, Jonathan, *Great Moments in Australian History* (Allen & Unwin, 2009)

Kipling, Rudyard, 'The White Man's Burden', *The New York Sun* (New York), 10 February 1899

Klimchuk, Marianne R and Sandra A Krasovec, *Packaging Design: Successful Product Branding from Concept to Shelf* (John Wiley & Sons, 2006)

Krippendorff, Klaus, *Content Analysis: An Introduction to its Methodology* (Sage Publications, 2nd ed, 2004)

'Ladies' Column: The Sewing Machine', *The Illustrated Sydney News and New South Wales Agriculturalist and Grazier* (Sydney), 26 October 1872, 4

Ladies Monthly Magazine, the World of Fashion, Journal of Fashion, Literature, Music, the Opera, and the Theatres (Simpkin, Marshall & Co, 1852-1879)

Lake, Jessica, *The Face that Launched a Thousand Lawsuits: The American Women who Forged a Right to Privacy* (Yale University Press, 2016)

'Law Report: Eno v Davies and Another', *Sydney Morning Herald* (Sydney), 11 June 1884, 6

Larson, Cedric, 'Patent-Medicine Advertising and the Early American Press' (1937) 14(4) *Journalism and Mass Communication Quarterly* 333

'Lecture on Temperance', *The Colonist* (Sydney), 25 June 1835, 3

Lever, James, *Fashions and Fashion Plates 1800-1900* (Penguin Books, 1943)

'Lewis and Whitty's Exhibit', *Australian Town and Country Journal* (Sydney), 27 April 1895, 22

Lewis, Milton, *A Rum State: Alcohol and State Policy in Australia 1788-1988* (AGPS Press, 1992)

'Lithographic Artists and Engravers' Club', *The Argus* (Melbourne), 22 February 1889, 4

'Lithographic Press', *The Australian* (Sydney), 24 October 1828, 4

'Little's "Phenyle"', *Sydney Morning Herald* (Sydney), 28 April 1892, 6

'Little's "Phenyle" Disinfectants', *The Argus* (Melbourne), 26 January 1899, 6

'Local Industries: Peacock's Jam Factory', *The Mercury Supplement* (Hobart), 12 February 1884, 1

Love, Peter, 'Melbourne Celebrates the 150th Anniversary of its Eight Hour Day' [2006] (91) *Labour History* 193

Marzio, Peter C, 'Lithography as a Democratic Art: A Reappraisal' (1971) 4(1) *Leonardo* 37

Maslen, Joan, 'Theatre Posters of the Golden Age' [1981] (21) *Australian Antique Collector* 65

Maslen, Joan, 'The Golden Age of Melbourne Theatre' (1995) 66(2) *Victorian Historical Journal* 137

Mason, Nicholas, *Literary Advertising and the Shaping of British Romanticism* (John Hopkins University Press, 2013)

'Melbourne Tea-Table Talk', *The West Australian* (Perth), 13 December 1886, 3

McClintock, Anne, *Imperial Leather: Race, Gender, and Sexuality in the Colonial Contest* (Routledge, 1995)

McClintock, Anne, 'Soft-Soaping Empire: Commodity Racism and Imperial Advertising' in N Mirzoeff (ed), *The Visual Cultural Reader* (Routledge, 1998)

McQuire, Scott, *Visions of Modernity* (Sage, 1997)

'Medical Testimonies', *The Teetotaller and General Newspaper* (Sydney), 5 March 1842, 4

'Messrs, Craig, Williamson, & Thomas's Establishment', Frearson's Monthly *Illustrated Adelaide News* (Adelaide), 1 March 1881, 35

'Messers. W.D. Peacock and Co's Jam Factory', *The Mercury* (Hobart), 7 March 1896, 3

'Moulton's Blood Searcher', *Burra Record* (South Australia), 14 May 1879, 4

'Moulton's Pain Paint', *The McIvor Times and Rodney Advertiser* (Heathcote), 8 May 1879, 1

'Moulton's Pain Paint', *Burra Record* (South Australia), 16 May 1879, 4

'Moulton's Pain Paint' (1884) 2(79) *The Bulletin* 21

'Mr H L Penfold Hyland, Wine Maker', *Advocate* (Burnie), 7 May 1940, 2

'Mr Ralph Potts Dies', *The Daily News* (Perth), 14 March 1944, 3

Muskett, Philip E, *The Art of Living in Australia* (Sydney University Press, first published 1893, 2016 ed)

Musson, A E, *Enterprise in Soap and Chemicals: Joseph Crosfield and Sons Ltd, 1815–1965* (Manchester University Press, 1965)

Naylor, Simon, 'Spacing the Can: Empire, Modernity, and the Globalisation of Food' (2000) 32 *Environment and Planning* A 1625

'New and Wonderful Discovery', *The Colonist* (Sydney), 11 December 1839, 4

'New Premises for the Melbourne Sports Depot', *Prahran Chronicle* (Melbourne), 3 May 1902, 3

Newson, Linda A, 'The Demographic Collapse of Native Peoples of the Americas, 1492-1650' (1993) 81 *Proceedings of the British Academy* 247

'New South Wales Album' (Charles Troedel & Co, 1878)

'Obituary: The Late Mr Charles Troedel', January 1907

Op den Kamp, Claudy and Hunter, Dan (eds) *A History of IP in 50 Objects* (Oxford University Press, 2019)

'Opera House', *The Argus* (Melbourne), 14 May 1883, 8

'Our Local Industries No. 5: W/D/ Peacock's Jam Factory', *The Tasmanian News* (Hobart), 5 August 1904, 3

'Patent Illuminating Map Printing', *South Australian* (Adelaide), 20 July 1841, 4

Petty, Ross D, 'From Label to Trademark: The Legal Origins of the Concept of Brand Identity in Nineteenth Century America' (2012) 4(1) *Journal of Historical Research in Marketing* 129

'Poisoning by Carbolic Acid', *Australian Town and Country Journal* (Sydney), 2 November 1872, 2

Prang, Louis, 'Art Critics Criticised' in Prang's *Chromo 1: A Journal of Popular Art* (L Prang and Company, 1868)

Prochaska, F K, *Women and Philanthropy in Nineteenth-Century England* (Clarendon Press, 1980)

'Publications and Literature', *The Argus* (Melbourne), 25 July 1863, 8

Raizman, David, *History of Modern Design* (Prentice Hall, 2nd ed, 2011)

'Ralph Potts Again', *The Goldfields Morning Chronicle* (Coolgardie), 15 November 1897, 3

Ramamurthy, Anandi, *Imperial Persuaders: Images of Africa and Asia in British Advertising* (Manchester University Press, 2003)

Rappaport, Erika, *A Thirst for Empire: How Tea Shaped the Modern World* (Princeton University Press, 2017)

'Registration of Ralph Potts', *The Menzies Miner* (Western Australia), 24 September 1898, 20

Reichert, Tom, *The Erotic History of Advertising* (Prometheus Books, 2003)

'Retirement Ends 65 Years' Printing', *The Age* (Melbourne), 26 April 1963, 4

Richardson, Megan, Klein, Jill and Thomas, Julian, 'From 'Omoo' to 'Oro': Nostalgia Labels and Cultural Policy on the Australian Trade Marks Register' in Susy Frankel (ed) The Object and Purpose of Intellectual Property (Edward Elgar, forthcoming)

Risch, Sara, 'Food Packaging History and Innovations' (2009) 57(18) *Journal of Agricultural and Food Chemistry* 8089

'Robert Harper and Co's Australian Manufactures', *The Queenslander* (Brisbane), 19 June 1897, 1352

'Robertson & Moffat', *Illustrated Australian News* (Melbourne), 3 October 1878, 176

Rosen, Zvi S, 'Reimagining Bleistein: Copyright for Advertisements in Historical Perspective' (2012) 59 *Journal of the Copyright Society in the USA* 347

Ruskin, John, *The Elements of Drawing* (George Allen, 1898)

Saggers, Sherry and Dennis Gray, *Dealing with Alcohol: Indigenous Usage in Australia, New Zealand and Canada* (Cambridge University Press, 1998)

Scardamaglia, Amanda, 'A Legal History of Lithography' (2017) 26(1) *Griffith Law Review* 1

Scardamaglia, Amanda, *Colonial Australian Trade Mark Law: Narratives in Lawmaking, People, Power and Place* (Australian Scholarly Publishing, 2015)

Scardamaglia, Amanda, 'Lithography' in Claudy Op den Kamp and Dan Hunter (eds) *A History of IP in 50 Objects* (Oxford University Press, 2019)

Shiell, Annette, *Fundraising, Flirtation and Fancywork: Charity Bazaars in Nineteenth Century Australia* (Cambridge Scholars Publishing, 2012)

'Science, Art, and Manufacturers: Lithographic Printing Press', *Adelaide Observer* (Adelaide), 7 February 1846, 2

Senefelder, Alois, *A Complete Course on Lithography* (A S trans, Ackermann, 1819)

Shaw, A G L, 'Some Aspects of New South Wales, 1788-1810' (1971) 57 *Journal of the Royal Australian Historical Society* 93

Sivulka, Juliann, *Soap, Sex, and Cigarettes: A Cultural History of American Advertising* (Cengage Learning, 2nd ed, 2012)

Smith, Bernard, *Place, Taste and Tradition: A Study of Australian Art Since 1788* (Oxford University Press, 2nd revised ed, 1979)

Snodgrass, Mary Ellen, *Encyclopedia of Kitchen History* (Fitzroy Dearborn, 2004)

Snodgrass, Mary Ellen, *World Clothing and Fashion: An Encyclopedia of History, Culture, and Social Influence* (Routledge, 2015)

Social Pages, *The Argus* (Melbourne), 26 June 1869, 4

Social Pages, *The Argus* (Melbourne), 11 September 1884, 5

Suzuki, Sarah, 'Toulouse-Lautrec: Life and Lithography', in *The Paris of Toulouse-Lautrec Prints and Posters from the Museum of Modern Art* (Museum of Modern Art, 2014) 9

Swanson, Kara W, 'Getting a Grip on the Corset: Gender, Sexuality and Patent Law' (2011) 23 *Yale Law Journal & Feminism* 57

Swanson, Kara W, 'Corset' in Claudy Op den Kamp and Dan Hunter (eds) *A History of IP in 50 Objects* (Oxford University Press, 2019)

The British Trade Journal & Export World, vol 20 (1 March 1882)

'The Celebrated Corset Case', *Ovens and Murray Advertiser* (Beechworth), 30 December 1905, 1

'The Colonel', *The Argus* (Melbourne), 10 April 1882, 6

'The Contributor: Notes Now and Then', *The Australasian* (Melbourne), 11 August 1883, 3

'The Corset Case', *Sunday Times* (Perth), 14 January 1906, 3

'The Corset Case', *Observer* (Adelaide), 16 June 1906, 43

'The Criterion Theatre', *Sydney Morning Herald* (Sydney), 7 May 1888, 8

'The Criterion Theatre', *Sydney Mail and New South Wales Advertiser* (Sydney), 12 May 1888, 1006

'The Curse of the Country', *Humbug*, 15 September 1869

'The Dental Board and Mr. Ralph Potts', *The West Australian* (Perth), 25 October 1898, 7

'The Great Corset Case', *The Sydney Morning Herald* (Sydney), 20 April 1905, 9

'The Opera-House Disaster', *Weekly Times* (Melbourne) 20 September 1884, 12

'The Patents' Copyrights Office, Melbourne', *Evening News* (Sydney), 17 January 1879, 3

'The Royal Society of Van Diemen's Land', *Launceston Examiner* (Launceston), 27 August 1851, 4

'The Story of Our Secondary Industries', *The Age* (Melbourne), 23 January 1937, 7

'The Vineyard: Introduction of Vine Grower's from the Continent', *The Farmer's Journal & Gardener's Chronicle* (Melbourne), 31 May 1862, 11

The World of Fashion and Continental Feuilletons (London, 1824-1851)

'To the Printer of the Sydney Gazette', *Sydney Gazette & New South Wales Advertiser* (Sydney), 12 November 1890, 2

'Trade Mark Application Number 520' in Victoria, *Victoria Government Gazette*, No 19, 16 February 1877, 362

'Tragedy at the Opera House', *The Brisbane Courier* (Brisbane), 2 August 1880

Tsara, Olga, 'Troedel & Co: Master Printers and Lithographers,' [1998] (62) *La Trobe Journal* 30

Turnbull, Clive (ed), 'The Melbourne Album': *Comprising a Series of Elegant, Tinted, Lithographic Views of Melbourne and Surrounding Districts Lithographed,*

Printed and Published by Charles Troedel in 1863 (Georgian House, 1961)

Twede, Diana, 'The Birth of Modern Packaging: Cartons, Cans and Bottles' (2012) 4(2) *Journal of Historical Research in Marketing* 245

Twede, Diana et al, *Cartons, Crates and Corrugated Board: Handbook of Paper and Wood Packaging Technology* (DEStech Publications Inc, 2nd ed, 2015)

'Typhoid Germs in Yan Yean Water', *The Argus* (Melbourne), 17 July 1889, 9

Tyrrell, Ian, 'The Anti-Tobacco Reform and the Temperance Movement in Australia: Connections and Differences' (1998) 84(1) *Journal of the Royal Australian Historical Society* 10

Paul Valéry, 'The Conquest of Ubiquity', in Jackson Matthews (ed) *The Collected Works of Paul Valéry, Aesthetics"* (Ralph Manheim trans, Pantheon Books, 1964)

Vannini, Phillip, *Material Culture and Technology in Everyday Life: Ethnographic Approaches* (Peter Lang, 2009)

Victorian Parliamentary Papers No. 11, 1860-61 (Melbourne, 1861)

Vinikas, Vincent, *Soft Soap, Hard Sell: American Hygiene in an Age of Advertisement* (Iowa State University Press, 1992)

Ward, Russel, *The Australian Legend* (Oxford University Press, 1981)

Westkaemper, Emily, *Selling Women's History: Packaging Feminism in Twentieth-Century American Popular Culture* (Rutgers University Press, 2017)

Williams, Raymond, *Keywords: A Vocabulary of Culture and Society* (Oxford University Press, 1976)

Young, James Harvey, *The Toadstool Millionaires: A Social History of Patent Medicines in America before Federal Regulation* (Princeton University Press, 2nd ed, 1972)

Cases

A-G (NSW) ex rel Tooth & Co Ltd v Brewery Employees' Union of NSW (1908) 6 CLR 469

Burgoyne's Trade Mark (1889) 6 RPC 227

CUB Pty Ltd v Elixir Signature Pty Ltd [2013] ATMO 74 (10 September 2013)

George Bleistein v Donaldson Lithographing Company, 188 US 239 (1903)

Intellectual Property Development Company Pty Ltd v CUB Pty Ltd [2013] ATMO 73 (10 September 2013)

Leather Cloth Co v American Leather Cloth (1865) 11 ER 1435

Re Weingarten Brothers (1903) 9 ALR 268a

Re Weingarten Brothers' Trade Mark (1904) 29 VLR 965

Scoville v Toland, 21 F Cas 863 (1848)

Sykes v Sykes (1824) 3 B & C 541; 107 ER 834

Weingarten Brothers v G & R Wills & Co [1906] SALR 34

Legislation

Dentists Act 1894 (WA)

Dentists Act 1898 (Vic)

Dentists Act 1900 (NSW)

Design and Trade Marks Act 1884 (WA)

Grant of Patents Act 1872 (WA)

Letters of Registration for Inventions Act 1852 (NSW)

Letters Patent for Inventions Act 1858 (Tas)

Merchandise Marks Act 1864 (Tas)

Patent Act 1856 (Vic)

Patents Act 1859 (SA)

Provisional Registration of Inventions Act 1867 (Qld)

Trade Marks Act 1863 (SA)

Trade Marks Act 1864 (Qld)

Trade Marks Act 1865 (NSW)

Trade Marks Registration Act 1876 (Vic)

Trade Marks Statute 1864 (Vic)

Treaties

Paris Convention for the Protection of Industrial Property, WO020EN (entered into force 20 March 1883)

Internet Sources

1854 Australia's First Biscuit Company Australian Food History Timeline <http://australianfoodtimeline.com.au/1854-australias-first-biscuit-company/>

Beaver, E A, Elliott, Sizar (1814-1901) Australian Dictionary of Biography <http://adb.anu.edu.au/biography/elliott-sizar-3478>

Bray, J J, Way, Sir Samuel James (1836-1916) Australian Dictionary of Biography <http://adb.anu.edu.au/biography/way-sir-samuel-james-9014>

Colligan, Mimi and Elisabeth Kumm, Opera House eMelbourne: The City Past & Present <http://www.emelbourne.net.au/biogs/EM01092b.htm>

Collingwood Historical Society Inc, Former Foy & Gibson Factory Buildings <http://collingwoodhs.org.au/resources/collingwood-history-plaques-project/former-foy-gibson-factory-buildings/>

Cook, Peter, Harper, Robert (1842 – 1919) Australian Dictionary of Biography <http://adb.anu.edu.au/biography/harper-robert-6572>

Dunstan, David, Brewers and Brewing eMelbourne: The City Past & Present <http://www.emelbourne.net.au/biogs/EM00232b.htm>

Fink, Elly, Young, William Blamire (1862–1935) Australian Dictionary of Biography <http://adb.anu.edu.au/biography/young-william-blamire-9218>

Forbes, M Z, Bannerman, Charles (1851-1930) Australian Dictionary of Biography <http://adb.anu.edu.au/biography/bannerman-charles-2929>

From Terra Australis to Australia State Library New South Wales <http://www.sl.nsw.gov.au/stories/terra-australis-australia/1808-rum-rebellion>

Gittins, Jean, Osborne, John Walter (1828-1902) Australian Dictionary of Biography <http://adb.anu.edu.au/biography/osborne-john-walter-4343>

Iltis, Judith, Boston, John (?-1804) Australian Dictionary of Biography <http://adb.anu.edu.au/biography/boston-john-1804>

Mercer, John, A Mark of Distinction: Branding and Trade Mark Law in the UK from the 1860s (27 July 2009) SSRN <http://ssrn.com/abstract=1439750>

Ministerial Council on Drug Strategy, Alcohol in Australia: Issues and Strategies (July 2001) Australian Government Department of Health, 1 <http://www.health.gov.au/internet/drugstrategy/publishing.nsf/Content/alc-strategy/%24FILE/alcohol_strategy_back.pdf>

Mitchell, Rebecca, '15 August 1862: The Rise and Fall of the Cage Crinoline' (2016) University of Birmingham Research Portal <https://research.birmingham.ac.uk/portal/files/29075836/Mitchell_Crinoline_Pre_Print.pdf>

Museums Victoria, Victorian Collections: Bottle: Phenyle <https://victoriancollections.net.au/items/5191b1ae2162ef064c6ef6d7>

Origins: Immigrant Communities in Victoria, History of Immigration from Germany Museum Victoria <https://museumvictoria.com.au/origins/history.aspx?pid=22>

Parker, Michelle I, The Truth is in the Lye: Soap, Beauty, and Ethnicity in British Soap Advertisements (History Undergraduate Thesis, Paper 7, University of Washington, 2014) <https://digitalcommons.tacoma.uw.edu/cgi/viewcontent.cgi?article=1008&context=history_theses>

Parsons, George, de Bavay, Auguste Joseph François (1856–1944) Australian Dictionary of Biography <http://adb.anu.edu.au/biography/de-bavay-auguste-joseph-francois-5934>

Penfolds History, Penfolds <https://www.penfolds.com/en-au/about-penfolds/heritage/our-history>

Rutledge, Martha, Joubert, Jules François de Sales (1824–1907) Australian Dictionary of Biography <http://adb.anu.edu.au/biography/joubert-jules-francois-de-sales-3874>

Smith, Bernard, Earle, Augustus (1793-1838) Australian Dictionary of Biography <http://adb.anu.edu.au/biography/earle-augustus-2016>

Stephens, Tillie and Liza K Dale-Hallett, Jam Factory – Factory & Companies Timeline (2008) Museum Victoria Collections <http://collections.museumvictoria.com.au/articles/2686>

Tout-Smith, Deborah, James Galloway, Leader of the Eight Hour Day Movement (1828-1860) Museums Victoria <https://collections.museumvictoria.com.au/articles/2099>

Troedel Archive, State Library Victoria <http://www.slv.vic.gov.au/search-discover/explore-collections-format/pictures/troedel-archive>

Victorian Heritage Database, Dights Mill Site (21 July 1999) Heritage Council Victoria <http://vhd.heritagecouncil.vic.gov.au/places/2>

Victorian Operative Masons' Society, Report of the Committee appointed by the Victorian Operative Masons' Society to inquire into the origin of the Eight-Hours' Movement in Victoria (Walker May Printers, 1884) <http://ergo.slv.vic.gov.au/explore-history/fight-rights/workers-rights/origins-8-hour-day> (adopted at the annual meeting on 11 June 1884)

Historical Artefacts and Advertising Material

Edward Gilks (1822-?), *Elizabeth Street* (1864) (Charles Troedel, Melbourne Album Office, 1864), State Library Victoria, H600

Edward Gilks (1822-?), *Flinders Street (From the Melbourne Railway Station)* (1864) (Charles Troedel, Melbourne Album Office, 1864), State Library Victoria, H3715

N K Fairbank Company Fairy Soap Advertisement, 'Why Doesn't Your Mamma Wash You with Fairy Soap' (c 1893) (Gray Lithograph Company, New York, 1893), Stanford Libraries, American Broadsides and Ephemera, First Series, 29523

Pears' Soap Advertisement, 'Pears Transparent Soap' (1884)

Pears' Soap Advertisement, 'The White Man's Burden' (1899), first published in *McClure's Magazine* (October 1899)

Robertson & Moffat Pty Ltd, *Wedding Gown* (Melbourne, 1892) National Gallery Victoria Accession Number D101-1971

The University of Melbourne Archives, *Robert Harper & Co Ltd* (1896–1982) Accession Number 82/104, 89/110

Victorian Heritage Database Report, *Former Carlton & United Brewery* (Victorian Heritage Register Number H0024)

Victoria Heritage Database Report, *Former Melbourne Sports Depot* (Hermes Number 64829)

Other

British Patent Number 1729 (22 July 1856)

British Patent Number 2518 (20 June 1801)

Trade Mark Numbers 1064 and 1065, *Victorian Trade Mark Register* (1885)

Trade Mark Numbers 2391-2394, *Victorian Trade Mark Register* (1890)

Trade Mark Number 9167, *Victorian Trade Mark Register* (1905)

United States Patent Number 8294 (12 August 1851)

US Patent Number US33517A (22 October 1861)

Index

Author Biography

Amanda Scardamaglia is an Associate Professor and Department Chair at Swinburne Law School. Amanda completed her LLB (Hons) and BA at The University of Melbourne before being admitted to practice as an Australian Legal Practitioner in the Supreme Court of Victoria. She has also completed her PhD in Law at The University of Melbourne. Amanda's area of research is intellectual property with a focus on empirical and historical studies in trade mark law, advertising, branding and the consumer. Amanda has published her work in a wide range of national and international peer-reviewed journals and has presented her work around the world. Amanda was a State Library of Victoria Creative Fellow in 2015-2016 and was awarded a residential fellowship at the Centre for Intellectual Property Policy & Management at Bournemouth University in 2017. She is the author of *Colonial Australian Trade Mark Law: Narratives in Lawmaking, People, Power and Place* (Australian Scholarly Publishing, 2015).

Published by Melbourne Books
Level 9, 100 Collins Street,
Melbourne, VIC 3000
Australia
www.melbournebooks.com.au
info@melbournebooks.com.au

Copyright © Amanda Scardamaglia 2020

All rights reserved. No part of this publication
may be reproduced, stored in a retrieval system,
or transmitted in any form or by any means without
the prior permission of the publisher.

Title: Printed on Stone: The Lithographs
of Charles Troedel
Author: Amanda Scardamaglia
ISBN: 9781925556490
Publisher: David Tenenbaum
Book design: Marianna Berek-Lewis, 5678 Design

NATIONAL
LIBRARY
OF AUSTRALIA

A catalogue record for this
book is available from the
National Library of Australia